Up & Running
with Windows 286/386

Up & Running
with Windows™ 286/386

Gabriele Wentges

San Francisco • Paris • Düsseldorf • London

Acquisitions Editor: Dianne King
Translator: Larry Childs
Supervising Editor: Eric Stone
Copy Editor: Richard Mills
Technical Editor: Dan Tauber
Word Processor: Deborah Maizels
Book Designer: Elke Hermanowski
Screen Graphics: Delia Brown
Typesetter: Ingrid Owen
Proofreader: Rhonda Holmes
Indexer: Nancy Anderman Guenther
Cover Designer: Kelly Archer

Windows is a trademark of Microsoft Corporation.
SYBEX is a registered trademark of SYBEX, Inc.

TRADEMARKS: SYBEX has attempted throughout this book to distinguish proprietary trademarks from descriptive terms by following the capitalization style used by the manufacturer.

SYBEX is not affiliated with any manufacturer.

Every effort has been made to supply complete and accurate information. However, SYBEX assumes no responsibility for its use, nor for any infringement of the intellectual property rights of third parties which would result from such use.

Library of Congress Card Number: 90-70023
ISBN: 0-89588-691-X

Manufactured in the United States of America
10 9 8 7 6 5 4 3 2 1

Up & Running

Let's say that you are comfortable with your PC. You know the basic functions of word processing, spreadsheets, and database management. In short, you are a committed and eager PC user who would like to gain familiarity with several popular programs as quickly as possible. The Up & Running series of books from SYBEX has been developed for you.

Who this book is for

This clearly structured guide shows you in 20 steps what the product can do, how you make it work, and how soon you can achieve practical results.

What this book provides

Your Up & Running book thus satisfies two needs: It describes the program's capabilities, and it lets you quickly get acquainted with the program's operation. This provides valuable help for a purchase decision. You also receive a 20-step basic course that provides a solid foundation in the program—even if you're a beginner with scant prior knowledge.

The benefits are plain to see. First, you will invest in software that meets your needs because, thanks to the appropriate Up & Running book, you will know the program's features and limitations. Second, once you purchase the product, you can skip the instruction manual and learn the basics of the program by following the 20 steps.

We have structured the Up & Running books so that the busy user spends little time studying documentation and the beginner is not burdened with unnecessary text.

Structure of the book

A clock shows your work time for each step. This indicates how much time you can expect to spend on each step with your computer.

*Required
time*

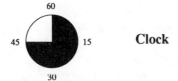

Clock

Naturally, you'll need much less time if you only read through the steps rather than carrying them out at your computer. You can also save some time by scanning the short notes in the margins to find the most important sections within a step.

Three symbols are used to highlight points of special note. These symbols and their meanings are shown below:

Symbols

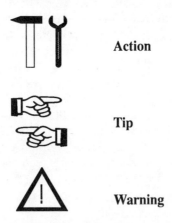

Action

Tip

Warning

An Up & Running book cannot, of course, replace a book or manual containing advanced applications. However, you will get the information needed to put the program to practical use and to learn its basic functions.

Contents

The first step always covers software installation in relation to hardware requirements. You'll learn whether the program can operate with your available hardware. Various methods for starting the program are also explained.

The second step introduces the program's user interface.

The remaining 18 steps demonstrate basic functions, using examples or short descriptions. You also learn about various facilities for printing data, displaying it on the screen, and importing and exporting it. The last steps cover special program features, such as a built-in macro language, additional editing facilities, or additional programs provided by third parties.

Steps 3–20

An Up & Running book will save you time and money.

SYBEX is very interested in your reaction to the Up & Running series. Your opinions and suggestions will help all of our readers, including yourself.

Preface

Windows is the computer cockpit from which you control all the capabilities of your computer with the push of a few buttons. Just like the pilot of a modern, sophisticated aircraft, the Windows user is visually guided quickly through the many functions with the help of graphic symbols.

Windows provides you with electronic versions of real office tools, such as the calendar, the cardfile, and the note pad. You use all these applications in the same intuitive way as you use Windows itself.

After giving you a quick overview of Windows, this book quickly teaches you the first applications. With its emphasis on essentials and its practice-oriented instructions, this book will have you using Windows for your daily work in no time at all.

Because of the forward-thinking Windows design, you have the same style of interface as both OS/2 and Unix/X/Windows. With only a little extra effort, you can master high-powered Windows-based programs for desktop publishing, spreadsheets, and word processing, such as PageMaker, Excel, and Word.

I hope that this book will spare you time-consuming study of the extensive original documentation, and I wish you fun and success with "windowing."

Gabriele Wentges, February 1990

Table of Contents

Step 1

Installation

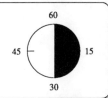

Before you begin using Windows, you must install and customize the program according to your computer's configuration. You use the Setup program, which installs Windows in a dialogue with you.

Hardware Requirements

Windows through version 2.0 runs on all PC compatibles (XT and AT computers), on 80386/486 computers, and on PS/2 systems.

Computer

For Windows 2.1 and up, special versions have been optimized for the 80286 and 80386 Intel processors. These versions, known as Windows/286 and Windows/386 respectively, run only on computers that are based on the corresponding processor. Upward compatibility has been maintained, so Windows/286 can be run on computers with the 80386 and 80486 processors.

You should have a graphics card that is Hercules, EGA, or VGA compatible and a flicker-free monitor with correspondingly high resolution. We don't recommend using a CGA card with a corresponding monitor. Windows also supports a number of full-page-display monitors.

Graphics card and monitor

In addition, you will need a hard disk with at least 2Mb of available storage space for serious work. To try out and test the system, however, one or two fast, high-density disk drives will suffice. We don't recommend your using low-density disk drives.

Hard disk

You can use almost any printer that supports paint fonts and graphics. Check with your dealer or with Microsoft to make sure that Windows is equipped to work with your printer.

Printer

Making Backup Copies

You should create copies of the Windows disks before you install them. If two disk drives are available, you can create a backup copy with the command

    DISKCOPY A: B:

If you have only one drive, use the command

    DISKCOPY A: A:

You will then be asked to exchange the disk in drive A with another one. Follow the directions on the screen until all the Windows disks have been copied.

Starting Setup

If you have
a hard disk

To install Windows, if you have a hard disk, insert the Windows Setup disk, containing the Setup program, in drive A. Start the installation by typing this command:

    SETUP

Press Enter. Windows determines which kind of graphics adapter, mouse, printer, and printer port, as well as which expanded memory system, are in use in your system. If you have a nonstandard graphics adapter, you will have to install the special Windows driver that has been included, according to the directions of the manufacturer.

Specify the drive where Windows should be installed and the name of the directory:

    C:\WINDOWS   or

    D:\WINDOWS

If you wish to run Windows in a system with two disk drives, type

If you have floppy disks

```
B:\WINDOWS
```

You need two blank high-density disks. However, by later deleting unnecessary applications, such as Reversi and printer fonts, you can copy your whole Windows system onto a single work disk.

After you indicate the disk drive and subdirectory, press Enter and follow the directions of the installation program. Windows will ask what type of computer you are using. Generally, the answer will be the default option, "AT and compatible." If so, then confirm it by pressing Enter. You can select another computer model by using the Down Arrow key.

Windows uses this information to determine which graphics adapter, keyboard, and type of mouse are present. If you see no errors in the specifications displayed, exit the installation program by pressing Enter.

Memory Expansion

Windows automatically recognizes certain types of expanded memory devices, such as the Intel or AST card and motherboards that have memory of more than 1Mb. If you have such a device, confirm the option by pressing Enter. Later, you may decide to allocate a portion of this additional storage space for use by the Windows program SMARTDrive. This program cooperates with Windows in reducing the amount of time your computer spends reading the hard disk.

If you have memory expansion not recognized by Windows, you must answer the question about memory expansion by choosing the option Other. If you do not have an expanded memory system, choose the option None. If you have an expanded memory system not supported by Windows, you will need to add this line to your CONFIG.SYS file for the driver delivered by the card manufacturer:

```
DEVICE = driver name
```

You will also need to copy the driver file into the root directory. You can use additional expanded memory with Windows at a later time by using the MS-DOS program MEM-SET.

Printers

Next, Windows asks you to select one or more printers for your print output from a list of supported printers.

It may be advantageous to include one printer under two selections on this list, if that printer can be run under two modes (for example, Epson or HP compatible). If you have a printer that is not included on the list of supported devices, ask the manufacturer to supply a driver if you don't have one. Then install the driver according to the manufacturer's directions.

You can also define additional printers later by using the Windows Control Panel.

You should now follow the rest of the Setup program directions, until Windows has installed all your disks.

Starting Windows

If you changed your AUTOEXEC.BAT file during installation, you must reboot your computer. Then you need only type the following:

```
WIN
```

Press Enter to start Windows. Otherwise, you must first change to the Windows directory by typing the following:

```
CD \WINDOWS
```

This works as long as you chose WINDOWS for the directory name, as we recommend. If you chose another name, such as WINDOWS.286, please note this in your user's manual.

Exiting Windows

You can leave Windows in one step by pressing Alt-F4 and then Enter.

Step 2
The User Interface

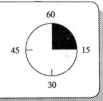

In the second step, we introduce you to one of the distinguishing features of Windows, the *user interface.*

The user interface of an application is characterized by the style of screen display and user controls. A good user interface supports you in your work and shields you from the complexity of the computer's underlying data processing.

Elements of the User Interface

Using Windows applications and communicating with Windows itself is straightforward. You can find your way around quickly in Windows since the screen display always has the same layout. Applications appear in open windows clearly visible on the screen or are represented by icons, which are small pictorial representations of application's whose windows are closed.

The Windows user interface makes working with objects easy. The selection of applications, input of commands, and editing of documents and graphics can largely be carried out by pointing and clicking with the mouse.

Application Windows

Each application is confined to a separate area of the screen, set off by its own border, or is represented by an icon. These separate areas, called windows, each have an independent set of control options and user interface elements.

You can also use commands that operate on the windows themselves, allowing you to open and close them, increase and decrease their size, move them on the screen, and switch between them. You can cut work from one application and paste it into another. You can run an application in the background, without entering or leaving it via the screen and without assigning it to any particular window.

Perhaps the easiest way for you to enter the Windows world is to think of Windows as an electronic desktop on which various folders, books, and note pads are located. The work materials are represented as applications windows. You can open and close them, stack them on top of each other, leaf through them, or make entries in them. Just as with paper materials, contents of applications windows can be cut, pasted, and copied.

In an electronic office, more work can be done, and done more rapidly and elegantly than by hand. Windows opens up possibilities that could never be conceived of in the paper world of the conventional office.

Step 3

The Windows Screen

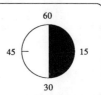

This step acquaints you with the very heart of Windows, the windows themselves. Using windows is a standard way of representing the input and output of applications on the screen.

All the applications windows in Windows are constructed in an identical manner from one unified set of structural elements. Not all the elements are present in every Windows application, and a few elements vary slightly from application to application.

It will be enough for now, however, if you understand the overall construction of Windows and the function of the individual elements when you have finished this step.

By way of example, let's look at a representation of a screen that comes up in the graphics application Corel Draw (see Figure 3.1). This example shows the clear structuring of Windows applications. You can see how individual windows can

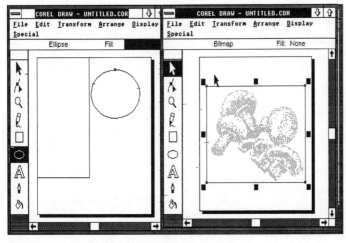

Figure 3.1: An applications window

be stacked on top of one other. This layered approach allows you to select individual drawings from one window and copy them into another one.

Window Elements

The Windows screen may contain one or more windows. (The maximum number is dependent on which applications you are running.) The typical layout of a screen is represented schematically in Figure 3.2.

1. The *window border* is part of the window, even when the window takes up the entire screen, and serves to delimit the window.

2. The *corner icon* is used to increase or decrease the size of the window (it does not show up in all windows).

3. The *title bar* contains the name of the window (4) and the window control boxes (5), (6), and (7).

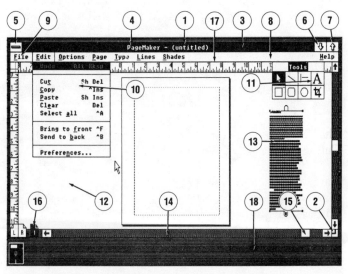

Figure 3.2: Schematic layout of Windows screen

4. The name of the application identifies the window.

5. The *Control-menu box* calls up the following options: Restore, Move, Size, Minimize, Maximize, Close. Other options may be on the Control menu of some applications.

6. The *Minimize box* (arrow pointing downward) reduces the window to an icon, but without terminating the application.

7. The *Maximize box* (arrow pointing upward) allows the window to fill the entire screen. When a window has been maximized, the box changes to the Restore box.

8. The *menu bar* is used to choose applications menus and to call up help functions. The menus available depend on the application you are using. As a rule, however, the File and Edit menus are always available.

9. The *File menu* always contains the following options: New, Load, Save, Print, About the Application, Exit.

Various applications offer these additional options: Execute, Information, Open, Load Associated Files, Save As, Save Area, Old Version, Convert, Close, Delete, Rename, Arrange Page, Position, Choose Printer, Configure Printer.

The *Edit menu* always contains the following options: Undo, Cut, Copy, Paste, Delete.

Various applications offer these additional options: Repeat, Mark All, Delete Contents, Paste Contents, Mark and Paste, Spaces, Fill Right, Fill Below, Place Ahead, Place Behind, Choose Handicap, Move Picture, Size Picture.

Besides File and Edit, the following additional menus are found in the menu bar: Options, Form, Text, Dates, Font

Style, Format, Macro, Window, Page, Lines, Area, Other, List, View, Search, Card, Undo, Size, Style, Palette, Paragraph, Goto, Alarm, Help.

10. The *drop-down menu*, sometimes called the pull-down menu, shows all items on the menu that can be selected. The items can be selected with the keyboard or with the mouse.

Keystroke combinations

Keystroke combinations are available to you for options you use frequently and are shown after the corresponding item on the menu. The drop-down menu is shown directly under the menu item to which it belongs; if the window is located near the bottom of the screen, the menu is shown above the item.

11. The *tools menu* has icons that graphically represent frequently used functions as pictographs. These icons represent tools found not only in the traditional office, such as a magnifying glass, a pencil, an eraser, scissors, a paintbrush, and glue, but also some that exist only in the electronic office.

For some applications, an edit line directly beneath the menu bar serves a function similar to the tools menu. For spreadsheet calculations, such as those found in Excel, you use the edit line to edit formulas and cell text.

12. This is an open work area in which text, graphics, and other objects to be edited can be shown, altered, and moved. In graphics applications, the objects may either partly or completely fill up the work area, which is also called the drawing or layout area.

13. This is a work area in which objects are being worked on. It could contain a page from a table, a document, a page with an illustration, a photo, text, or a portion of text.

14. The horizontal and vertical *scroll bars* position the visible portions of objects that project beyond the area of the window in a horizontal or vertical direction.

15. The highlighted squares on the scroll bars, known as *scroll boxes*, move along the bars and show the relative position of the visible portion of the object.

16. *Page icons* (not available in every application) allow you to leaf through documents that are several pages long. The current page is highlighted. You can also move directly to another page with page icons. These icons are located to the left of the horizontal-picture scroll bar.

Instead of using page icons, several applications use a page bar underneath the horizontal run bar, in which the current page number is shown. This page bar is used by Excel and other programs to communicate short messages.

17. *Rulers* support work for which precise measurements are important. They are shown in gray at the left and upper edges of the work area. Rulers are often complemented by corresponding rastering of the work area so that you can position your cursor anywhere in the work area.

Instead of using rulers and rastering, many applications structure the work area into lines and columns.

18. The *communications bar* displays short messages about mode and program status. If present, this line is found directly above the bottom border of the screen.

Examples of Applications Windows

Reversi

The game Reversi, which comes with your Windows package, offers a simple example of a window (see Figure 3.3).

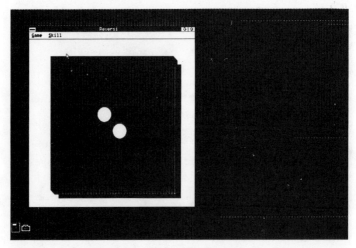

Figure 3.3: Applications window for Reversi

The objects you work with are the playing board and the game tokens you place on it. The board is found in the middle of the work area and is surrounded by a border. The name Reversi appears in the title bar. To the left is the Control-menu box, and to the right are the sizing icons.

The menu bar contains the two menus Game and Skill.

The drop-down menu Game includes these menu items: Hint, Messages, Pass, New, Exit, About Reversi.

The drop-down menu Skill offers the following levels of difficulty: Beginner, Novice, Expert, Master. At the level of master, the computer plays at the highest level of difficulty.

Dialog Boxes

When you call up the option About Reversi from the Game menu, a so-called dialog box with version and copyright information is superimposed on the window (see Figure 3.4).

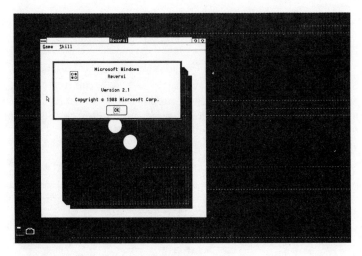

Figure 3.4: Dialog box in Reversi

Dialog boxes are windowlike areas that cannot be altered by
the user. They usually contain short messages and ask you to
respond to a multiple-choice option list. In our example your
only possible answer is OK, but other questions could also
take the answers Yes, No, or Cancel.

A dialog box is an important part of an applications window;
the questions in them must be answered before you can do
any more work in the window. Dialog boxes appear primarily
in error situations or when a large number of settings are necessary before you can begin a certain phase of editing.

Child Windows

Dependent child windows, sometimes called document windows, can appear inside a window. These windows belong to
the same program as the parent, or application, window, and
cannot exist without the parent. If the parent window is
closed, the child windows will also be closed.

Child windows can be opened, closed, altered, and moved like normal windows, responding to similar commands.

The Excel application, a spreadsheet program, makes extensive use of subwindows. These allow the simultaneous display of different spreadsheet areas for large-scale calculations, as well as the display of results and notes on individual formulas and data fields (see Figure 3.5).

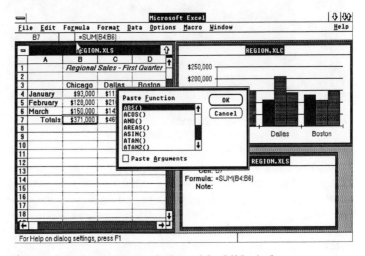

Figure 3.5: Applications window with child windows

Types of windows

In the example in Figure 3.5, the evaluation of a regional marketing statistical report is shown by a spreadsheet window, a child window with a bar chart, and a notepad window for the spreadsheet. A dialog box is superimposed on this, which allows a function to be selected for the field B7. The spreadsheet window in our Excel example has horizontal and vertical scroll bars. The work area is divided into lines and columns.

For another example of a typical window, look at Figure 3.6, where the PageMaker application is displayed.

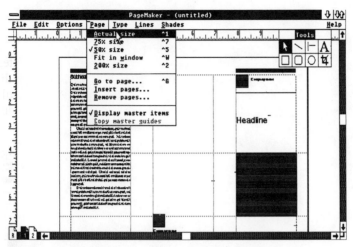

Figure 3.6: Applications window with PageMaker

The work area of PageMaker contains rulers with line and column markers. A graphics function menu offers various layout functions. All the pages of the document in the work area can be immediately selected by using the page icons.

PageMaker uses the rest of the work area as a clipboard for text and images of the document being edited, as you can see from the portion of text visible to the left of the document.

Step 4
Managing Windows

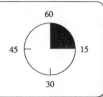

In this step we show you how Windows supports simultaneous work on several applications. Windows not only allows you to display several child windows within the same application but also allows you to display several different parent windows at the same time, each with a different application.

Sizing Windows

In Windows, you can make a window take up the entire screen by itself, or you can decrease its size so that it takes up only a portion of the screen. The example in Figure 4.1 shows the window for the Clock application on an otherwise empty screen.

Using the Maximize Box

You can expand the Clock window to fill the entire area of the screen by using the Maximize box in the title bar (see Figure 4.2).

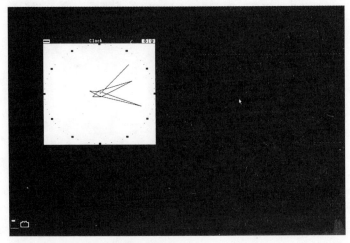

Figure 4.1: The Clock application

Using the Minimize Box

When you select the Minimize box, the Clock window disappears, and nothing is visible on the screen but two icons (see Figure 4.3). One of the icons looks like a disk and represents the MS-DOS application; the other icon represents the window for the Clock application, which is now closed.

The icons for applications that are currently present in Windows, but whose windows are closed, are placed off to the side on the lower-left edge of the Windows screen. They may be moved around as you see fit.

By choosing an application's icon, you can reopen its window. You have the option of opening the window at its former size, at the standard size (this varies according to the application), or at a larger size.

Running Multiple Windows

More than one window can appear on the Windows screen. In Figure 4.4, several Calculator and Clock windows are visible.

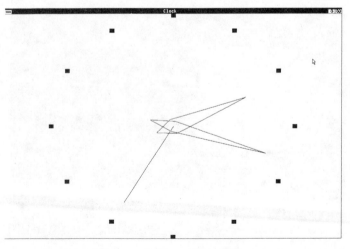

Figure 4.2: The Clock application as a full screen

It may not be helpful to display several clocks on the screen at the same time, but this example demonstrates that several applications can run simultaneously. For many applications it

Figure 4.3: Screen with two icons

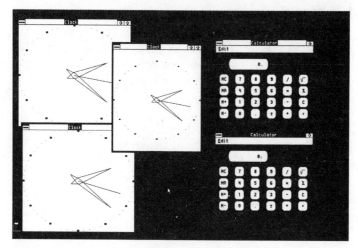

Figure 4.4: Several applications windows

may be practical for you to run several copies of the same application, using each one for a different task.

Making a window active

When several applications are present simultaneously in open windows on the screen, you need to know which window you can use. Only one window at a time is active. The active window can carry on a dialog with you, send messages, display results, and receive commands. It is designated by a dark background on its title bar. You can select a specific window with the mouse or by pressing a key.

You can expand or compress a window by dragging the corner icons or window borders with the mouse pointer or by using the direction keys on the keyboard.

Moving windows

You can also move a window around on the screen by dragging the title bar with the mouse or by using the direction keys. In doing this, windows will sometimes overlap. If you select a partly covered window with the mouse or the keyboard, it will automatically be placed on the top of the stack of windows.

The active window is always found in the foreground, covering the windows that are located in the same area on the screen (see Figure 4.5). You can get to the covered windows by leafing through the ones on top, using keyboard commands. Alternatively, you can diminish the size of, or remove altogether, the windows on top.

The imaginary surface on which windows can be moved around is greater than what is displayed on the Windows screen. You can move windows horizontally and vertically off the screen.

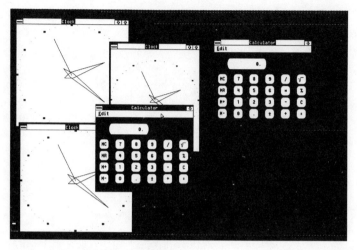

Figure 4.5: Overlapping windows

Step 5

Starting and Ending

Now that you are comfortable with the Windows user interface, in this step you begin to learn some of its practical applications. First, you will learn how to start and end Windows and Windows applications.

Starting Windows

You should have installed Windows on a hard disk and adapted the AUTOEXEC.BAT file so that Windows can be started with the WIN command. Now perform the following steps:

1. Turn your PC on, and if necessary, enter the date and the time. Your computer will display the prompt C>.

We will represent a sequence of keys by separating the corresponding key names with commas, for example, Enter, Enter. This tells you to press the Enter key twice.

Key sequence

When you are asked to press two keys at the same time, we will put a hyphen between them, for example, Alt-F4. This combination tells you to press the function key F4 while you hold down the Alt key.

Key combination

2. Type the following command to start Windows after the prompt:

    WIN

    or

    WIN/386

Press Enter.

3. Confirm the command by pressing Enter again. After a few moments, the Microsoft logo will appear on the screen. Windows starts with the MS-DOS Executive application window open.

Possible Problems and Solutions

If you have not installed Windows so that it can be started directly by entering WIN or WIN/386, then do the following:

1. After the C prompt, enter the name of the drive where you have installed Windows, followed by a colon:

    `C>A:`

    or

    `C>B:`

Press Enter.

2. Change to the proper subdirectory:

    `CD \WINDOWS`

If the "Invalid Directory" message appears, check to see if you chose another directory name when you installed Windows, and use that name instead. If you cannot remember the name, then look at the directory listing on the current disk by typing the following command:

    `DIR \P`

Press Enter. You can page forward in the directory listing by pressing the spacebar. Subdirectories are indicated by the presence of DIR behind the name. The date and time of your creation of the directory are included.

3. Call up Windows by typing

   WIN

Press Enter. Unless you have set it up otherwise, the application MS-DOS Executive window (described in detail in Step 14) will appear first after Windows is started. You can start other applications from this window.

Starting an Application

There are several ways you can call up an application:

1. You can select the name of the application with the mouse or the arrow keys.

2. You can type the initial letter of the application's name.

Initial letter

Selection bar

Using the Clock application as an example, type the initial letter, C. If this application is not the first one that starts with C, press the letter key repeatedly until the selection bar is over the CLOCK.EXE file. Press Enter, and the Clock window appears.

Closing a Window

You can close the Clock window by pressing Alt-F9. The Clock icon will appear on the lower border of the screen.

Opening a Window

The active window is indicated by the dark background of the title bar. The first Clock application was temporarily represented by its icon, but it becomes active again when you choose its icon. A superimposed title bar along the lower edge of the icon indicates that it is active.

1. Press Alt-Esc twice.

2. Open the Clock application by pressing Alt-F5.

Two clocks now appear on the screen (see Figure 5.1).

3. Activate the MS-DOS Executive window again to start another application by pressing Alt-Esc twice.

Starting an Application Indirectly

Windows offers you the option of starting an application indirectly by loading a file that was already created with that application. This helps you because you don't need to enter extra commands to load both the file you're going to work on and the application.

This option is possible because of a three-character file name extension that is automatically added when the file is saved

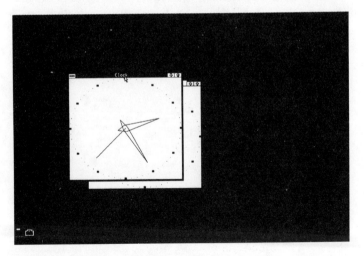

Figure 5.1: Two Clock applications

and is associated with an application. For example, a file with the name TEXT.WRI was created by the Windows application Write.

The file name extension for each application is listed in the Windows system file WIN.INI.

The extension .WRI for the Write application and .MSP for the Paint application are predefined and serve as examples. You can make additional entries yourself.

1. Press the W key until you have selected the WIN.INI entry.

2. Press Enter to load the application.

You edit files having the .INI extension with the Windows application Notepad. Pressing the Enter key both starts the Notepad application and loads the WIN.INI file.

All lines in this file that begin with a semicolon contain comments that have no further effect. You should include comments when you make changes.

3. When the Notepad appears, press the PgDn key until you can see the following entries:

    ```
    ini=notepad.exe ^.ini
    msp=paint.exe ^.msp
    wri=write.exe ^.wri
    ```

4. At this spot, you can add more entries for additional applications or change existing entries. For example, if you wish to work with Word under Windows, then change the line

    ```
    txt=notepad.exe ^.txt
    ```

    to

    ```
    txt=word.com ^.txt
    ```

To do this, use the arrow keys to move the blinking vertical bar, which shows where the text you type will be inserted, to the desired position. Type in the new information. You can delete old text with the Del key.

Now when you load files with the .TXT extension, Windows will start Word instead of the Notepad application.

5. If you want to include the PageMaker application, then add the following lines:

```
pm3=pm.exe ^.pm3
pt3=pm.exe ^.pt3
```

You can add program names and extensions for most Windows applications to this list in Notepad. You will find more about using the Notepad application in Step 11.

Starting an Application Automatically

When you start Windows, you can start other, previously chosen, applications along with it. The Clock application is a good choice for this because it requires only 15K of memory.

You start the application by modifying the WIN.INI file, which should still be present on your screen.

1. Press the PgUp key once so that the following lines from the WIN.INI file appear on the screen:

```
load=
run=
```

You can enter a list of applications, separated by spaces, after these two parameters to load these applications automatically when Windows is started.

You should list applications that you want started as open windows after the run line. You should list applications that you want started as icons after the load line.

2. As an example, have the Clock start as an icon. Enter "clock" after the load line:

    ```
    load=clock
    ```

3. To save your change by writing it to the disk, call up the File menu by pressing Alt-F.

    Saving changes

4. Select the Save option by typing the letter S. From now on, the Clock icon will appear at the bottom of the screen when you start Windows.

Starting the Windows Program Automatically

If you plan to work primarily with Windows and applications under Windows, you can change the system file AUTOEXEC.BAT so that Windows is automatically started when you turn on your computer.

This works only if no other applications, especially menu applications, are set up to start automatically when the system is started. Otherwise, you first need to remove any such applications from the AUTOEXEC.BAT file. The AUTOEXEC.BAT file must be located in the root directory of the boot drive.

1. Pull down the File menu in the notepad that is displaying the WIN.INI file by pressing Alt-F.

2. Select the Open command, O. The dialog box for opening files belongs to the Notepad application.

3. Press the Backspace key three times to delete the .TXT extension in the parameter field.

4. Type the character sequence "bat."

5. Press Enter and then the Tab key. This puts you in the directory listing offered by the dialog box.

6. To switch to the root directory, where the AUTO-EXEC.BAT file is located, move the highlight to the entry, and press Return. Now your screen should look like Figure 5.2.

7. Press the Enter key, which loads all of your files with a .BAT file extension into the root directory.

8. Press the A key repeatedly to select the AUTO-EXEC.BAT file, and then press Enter to load it into the Notepad application.

9. Move the insertion point to the first free line at the end of the displayed text, and type WIN or WIN/386.

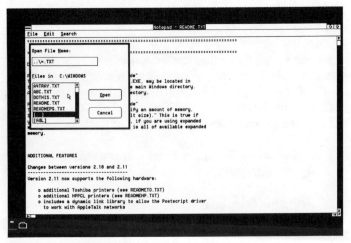

Figure 5.2: Loading a file

Ending an Application

You can save any changes you have made before leaving an application by pressing the standard Alt-F, S. However, if you forget to do this, Windows will remind you.

1. End the Notepad application by pressing Alt-F4. A dialog box appears, asking if you want to save the AUTOEXEC.BAT file.

2. Answer Yes by pressing Y. From now on, Windows will automatically be called up as soon as the system is started.

Exiting Windows

1. Press the key combination Alt-F4. A dialog box appears, asking for confirmation with OK.

2. Make sure OK is highlighted, and press Enter to confirm your selection.

This procedure also closes any other applications and windows that are present. Windows will alert you if any of the applications contain files that have been changed but not saved. You have to exit all non-Windows applications before you can exit Windows.

In the next two steps, we tell you in more detail about how to run Windows using the mouse and the keyboard. This will help you run the applications that are presented in later steps.

Step 6

Using the Mouse

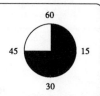

This step introduces you to using Windows with a mouse. In almost all situations, you will find using the mouse to be the most intuitive and comfortable way to control Windows.

Mouse Functions

You can run Windows using the left mouse button and only four different mouse control functions. (You can use another mouse button by making a change in the CONTROL.EXE application, which we introduce later.)

The following is a list of general mouse control functions (they may not necessarily work in all applications):

1. *Pointing*: Move the mouse on the pad so that the diagonal arrow points to an object on the Windows screen.

2. *Selecting or clicking*: Point to an object, and press the left mouse button.

3. *Choosing or double-clicking*: Point to an object, and press the left mouse button twice.

The amount of time Windows allows you between the two clicks can be customized in the CONTROL.EXE application to meet your needs.

4. *Dragging*: While holding the mouse button down, move the pointer over a list, over sections of text, or over individual graphic objects.

5. *Marking*: Click on the selection bar, or drag it over a list or sections of text, or stretch a selection area over part of a graphic object by holding the left mouse button down.

Mouse Objects

The objects that can be addressed by the mouse are window elements that were introduced to you in Step 3:

- Window border
- Corner icon
- Title bar
- Control-menu box
- Minimize box
- Maximize box
- Menus in the menu bar
- Highlighted menu options
- Icon graphics in a function menu
- Editing line
- Work area
- Objects and symbols in the work area
- Scroll boxes and direction arrows in a scroll bar
- Page icons
- Fields or raster objects in a structured work area

You can also click on text entries in lists, text boxes, command buttons in dialog boxes, color fields, sample fields, and letter symbols.

Running Windows Efficiently

You will find that it may not be best or even possible to use your mouse in every situation. In some cases, you may find it more practical to use a combination of keyboard commands and mouse controls or just the keyboard commands.

Manipulating Windows

Now let's practice with the mouse. Start Windows, as described in Step 5. The MS-DOS Executive window is open.

Changing the Size of a Window

As an exercise, let's change the size of the MS-DOS Executive window in several different ways:

1. Point to the upper-left corner of the screen so that the corner-arrow icon changes into a two-headed arrow. Drag the icon diagonally downward to the right. This makes the MS-DOS Executive window smaller. (The icon remains a two-headed arrow until you release the mouse button.)

2. Point to the lower-right corner, and drag the arrow diagonally downward to the right until you reach the edge of the screen. The MS-DOS Executive window grows larger.

3. Drag the right border inward until it won't go any farther. The MS-DOS Executive window gets so small that, if you have more than two disk drives; the drive symbols take up more than one line. You will see a scroll bar along the lower edge of the screen.

Changing the Position of a Window

Drag the title bar upward and to the right with the mouse so that the MS-DOS Executive window is placed precisely in the upper right-hand corner of the Windows screen.

Scrolling the Contents of a Window

Drag the scroll box to the right edge of the horizontal scroll bar. The Windows directory display moves to the right, as pictured in Figure 6.1.

Working with Files

Let's see how to perform file operations with the mouse. Mark the WRITE.EXE application and double-click.

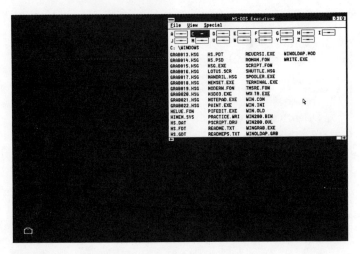

Figure 6.1: Scrolling a window

Opening a File

We now want to open a file inside the Write application.

1. Click on the File menu. This menu contains all the necessary commands for working with files. Besides the Control menu, this is the most important menu; it is used in almost all applications.

2. Click on the menu option Open.

3. Select the file PRACTICE.WRI from the director listing in the dialog box, and open it with a double click (see Figure 6.2).

Saving a File

After you make changes to a file, you can save them by doing the following:

1. Click on the Save option in the File menu. All the changes you have made will be written into the file

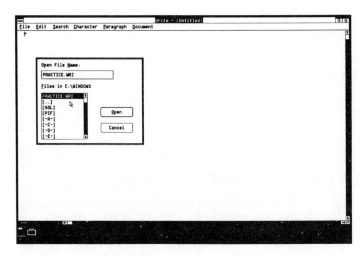

Figure 6.2: Opening a file

PRACTICE.WRI. The previous contents of the file are erased.

2. If you don't want the original text to be written over, you can save changed text under a different name. To do this, click on the Save As option in the File menu.

3. A dialog box appears, and you can enter the new name. When you type the first letter, it automatically deletes the old name. When you're done, click on the OK command button. (If you omit the file name extension, Write will use .WRI by default.)

Changing file names

If you make a mistake when you enter the new name, you can cancel it by pressing Esc.

Printing a File

Click on the Print command in the File menu, and then click on the OK command button in the dialog box that pops up.

Wait for a short time until the dialog box disappears by itself. The file prints.

Reading Messages

The last option in the File menu is usually reserved for short messages about an application, in this case, About Write. Click on this option with the mouse.

Working with Multiple Windows

For the following exercises keep the Write window active. Drag the right border of the window to the left until the MS-DOS Executive window is completely visible again.

Making a Window Active

Click on the MS-DOS Executive window with the mouse to make this window active again. The title bar of the Write window turns gray, signifying that the window is no longer active.

Changing to Another Drive

Make sure there is a formatted, nonempty disk in drive A. Click on the A drive symbol in the MS-DOS Executive work area. The directory listing for the disk in drive A appears in the MS-DOS Executive window.

Scrolling a Window's Contents

You can scroll through the directory listing by repeatedly clicking on the right scroll arrow.

Changing between Icon and Standard Window

1. Double click on the Clock icon in the lower-left corner. The Clock window will overlap the Write window (see Figure 6.3).

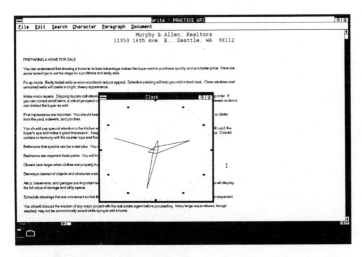

Figure 6.3: Overlapping windows

2. Click on the Write window so it becomes active again. It will now overlap the Clock window.

3. End the Write application by using the Control menu. Click on the Control-menu box, the small cross beam to the left of the title bar, and then click on the menu command Close. If you made any changes to the file, you will be asked to save them before the Write application is closed.

Ending the application

4. To change the clock back to an icon, click on the Minimize box, the down arrow to the right of the title bar.

Changing between Full Screen and Standard Window

After you have completed these steps, change the MS-DOS Executive window to full-screen representation. Click on the Maximize box, the up arrow to the right of the title bar. You can return to the previous display mode by repeatedly clicking the mouse.

Ending Windows

To end a Windows session, click on the File menu and select the Exit option. Confirm this by clicking on the OK command button. (The File menu is found in the menu bar of almost all applications.)

You can also end Windows by selecting the Close option in the Control menu.

Windows /386

In Windows/386, the Settings option in the Control menu provides you with an emergency exit. This should only be used, however, when the application will not respond to any other commands.

After you choose this menu option, a dialog box appears with the following options:

    Display Options
    Execution
    Tasking Options

Display Options allows you to switch the window mode of a standard MS-DOS application between standard size and full-screen representation.

Execution allows you to temporarily suspend an application or to resume an application that has been suspended.

Tasking Options allows you to decide whether you want to work in foreground, background, or exclusive mode. Foreground mode lets the application run only when it is active. Background mode lets the application run whether or not it is active. Exclusive mode allows one application that is active to run by itself.

Step 7
Using the Keyboard

This step introduces you to the operation of the keyboard. You can execute Windows commands very quickly once you have memorized the keyboard shortcuts for each action. If, however, you are an occasional user or a beginner who relies on calling up menus, using the mouse is definitely easier. Also, seldom-used Windows functions have no keyboard shortcuts.

Calling Up a Menu

You can call up a menu for a window by pressing the Alt key plus one additional key at the same time. The additional key for each menu is indicated by an underlined letter in the menu name.

In the MS-DOS Executive window, for example, you can reach the

- File menu via the key combination Alt-F
- View menu via the key combination Alt-V
- Special menu via the key combination Alt-S

You can access the Control menu via Alt-spacebar or Shift-Esc. As you already know, this menu is symbolized by a small cross beam in the title bar.

Every option whose name contains an underlined letter can be accessed by pressing that letter. However, for menu names in the menu bar, you must also press the Alt key.

An Exercise in Calling Up Menus

1. Start Windows as described in Step 5, if you have not already done so.

2. Select the File menu by pressing Alt-F. Besides the Control menu, the File menu is the most important because it contains all the options for working with files.

3. Once the File menu appears, you can choose a menu option in one of three different ways:

   • Use the arrow keys to highlight an option and press Enter
   • Press the Alt key plus a function key (for some options)
   • Press the underlined letter in an option

4. Press the letter B to select the About MS-DOS Exec option in the open File menu. You will see a dialog box with information about free space on the disk and in memory.

5. Press the Enter key to confirm that you have read the message. The dialog box disappears.

Loading an Application

Next, load an application via the File menu.

1. Press Alt-F and then L. After you choose the Load menu option, a dialog box appears.

2. Enter the name of the Clock application in the text box, and leave the field by pressing Tab.

3. If you set up the clock application to start automatically as described in step 5, the Clock icon already appears in the lower-left corner of the screen. To get rid of it, press Tab to call up the Cancel button, then press Enter.

4. Otherwise, start the Clock application as an icon by selecting the OK button and pressing Enter.

Selecting Menus

Let's do a few exercises in calling up menu options.

If you have called up the Special menu by pressing Alt-S, and now want to open up the View menu, you can switch from one menu to the other by using the arrow keys inside the menu bar.

1. Change from the Special menu to the View menu by using the Left Arrow key. This menu allows you to change the way the directory listing in the MS-DOS Executive window is displayed.

2. Choose the Long display mode by pressing the Down Arrow key once and Enter. The appearance of the directory list will change. Additional information such as size and creation date and time will now be displayed.

Now let's look at the special Control menu, which appears in every Windows application.

The Control Menu

You can open the Control menu, which is displayed to the left of the title bar as a small cross beam, by using the keyboard combination Alt-spacebar. At first, using the menu is the simplest method, but to get to your most important functions, the menu is too slow.

Here is a quicker method that the experts use.

Shortcuts for Control Menu Functions

In addition to choosing Control menu functions by using direction keys in the menu, you can also get to them directly with the keyboard combination of the Alt key and a function key, without first having to open the menu.

The functions described in Table 7.1 all work in a currently active window.

Key Combination	Function
Alt-F4	End an application
Alt-F5	Restore a window to standard size
Alt-F7	Move a window
Alt-F8	Change window size
Alt-F9	Switch from standard size to icon display (Minimize)
Alt-F10	Switch from standard size to full-screen display (Maximize)

Table 7.1: Shortcuts for Control Menu Options

Other applications use combinations of the Alt key plus the F1, F2, F3, F6, F11, and F12 function keys.

An Exercise in Using Control Function Shortcuts

Once you have opened any one of the four MS-DOS Executive menus—the Control menu and the File, View, and Special menus—you can move to any of the others with the Left Arrow and the Right Arrow keys. You can use Esc to leave the menu level.

Now let's practice calling up the Control menu functions.

1. Use the Alt-F10 combination to change the size of the MS-DOS Executive window from standard size to full-screen representation.

2. Use the Alt-F9 combination to change the window from standard size to icon representation.

3. Use the Alt-F8 combination to change the size of the window. A four-headed arrow appears, which you can place on the right window border by using the Right Arrow key. Hold the Left Arrow key down until the right window border moves to the middle of the screen. Press Enter to confirm your action.

4. Use the Alt-F7 combination to change the position of the window. Again, a four-headed arrow appears, which you can place on the right window border by using the Right Arrow key. Hold the Right Arrow key down until the MS-DOS Executive window is at the right edge of the screen. Press Enter to confirm your action.

If you are in a hurry, you can skip the next three sections for now, and go directly to the "Working in Windows" section.

Shortcuts for File Menu Functions

In addition to combinations of Alt and a function key, some applications also use combinations of Ctrl and a function key. Using the Ctrl combinations described in Table 7.2, you can

Key Combination	Function
Ctrl-D	Place an object
Ctrl-P	Print an object
Ctrl-N	Create a new file
Ctrl-O	Open a file
Ctrl-S	Save an object in the work area

Table 7.2: Shortcuts for File Menu Options

directly access functions in the File menu of PageMaker and other applications without having to call up the menu.

In the MS-DOS application, the combination of the Ctrl key and a letter has a special meaning. You use it to access the disk drive designated by that letter. Ctrl-A, for example, accesses drive A.

Moving Objects between Applications

As you have already seen, every application window has a Control menu, and most windows also have a File menu.

Because Windows allows you to move objects, such as text, drawings, and pictures, between applications using a clipboard, you can use shortcuts in most applications to do this more easily.

Graphics-oriented applications offer you three shortcuts for exchanging objects: Copy, Cut, and Paste. Applications that primarily receive graphics, but do not produce them, usually support only the Paste and Copy functions.

Step 16, which discusses the Clipboard application, provides you with a useful example of how to bring objects into one application from another application.

The functions described in Table 7.3 always apply to the selected area in the application when they are first called up. You can always expand this default selection to cover a larger area.

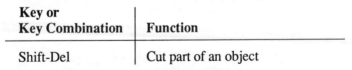

Key or Key Combination	Function
Shift-Del	Cut part of an object

Table 7.3: Shortcuts for Transferring Objects

Key or Key Combination	Function
Ctrl-Ins	Copy all or part of an object to the Clipboard
Shift-Ins	Paste all or part of an object from the Clipboard
Del	Delete all or part of an object
Esc	Restore a selected area after a Copy or Cut command

Table 7.3: Shortcuts for Transferring Objects (cont.)

Shortcuts for Terminal Operation

Windows reserves additional key combinations for terminal operations with other computers, using the TERMINAL.EXE application in the MS-DOS Executive window. These are described in Table 7.4.

Key Combination	Function
Alt-F3	Dial a phone number you specified in the Configure menu to connect your computer automatically with another computer
Ctrl-F4	Print data from another computer at the same time it appears on the screen
Ctrl-F5	Save the currently displayed data in a file called NAME.TXT, or save the selected terminal options in a file called NAME.TRM

Table 7.4: Shortcuts for Terminal Options

Key Combination	Function
Ctrl-F6	Interrupt the incoming data stream, with the danger of data loss if an XOn/XOff protocol is not used
Ctrl-F7	Terminate the computer connection (sends a break signal to the other computer)

Table 7.4: Shortcuts for Terminal Options (cont.)

Working in Windows

You can use basic key functions in Windows to select, choose, and manipulate objects in windows, functions in dialog boxes, and entries in lists.

Applications developed especially for Windows use function keys with special uses beyond the basic key functions listed in Tables 7.5 and 7.6. You will learn these special uses in the steps that cover those applications.

Key	Function
Home	Place the insertion point at the beginning of a line, or select the first list entry
End	Place the insertion point at the end of a line, or select the last list entry
Arrow Keys	Select an individual object, and position the insertion point
Tab	Move within a dialog box
Ins	Turn insertion mode on and off

Table 7.5: Basic Key Functions

Key	Function
Spacebar	Change the selection mode: switch marker to light or dark; delete entry field
PgUp, PgDn	Page through lists, and scroll through objects
Esc	Cancel an action or a dialog, and close a menu or a dialog box
Enter	Choose an object; confirm a default option like OK; load an application from an open MS-DOS Executive window; execute a command
Letter	Select an object whose name contains the letter
Backspace	Delete a character to the right of the insertion point
Del	Delete a character to the left of the insertion point; delete all selected text

Table 7.5: Basic Key Functions (cont.)

Key	Function with Shift	Function with Alt
Home	Select from the insertion point to the beginning of the line	
End	Select from the insertion point to the end of the line	
Arrow	Select groups of objects, and drag the marker	
Tab	Select dialog fields in reverse order	Change the active window

Table 7.6: Key Combinations with Shift and Alt

Key	Function with Shift	Function with Alt
Ins	Receive an object from the Clipboard	
Spacebar		Call up the Control menu
PgUp, PgDn	Select groups of objects	
Esc	Select the Control menu	Change the active window
Enter		Change between the standard MS-DOS display and Windows display for an application under Windows/386; print screen (hard copy) for CGA video mode
Letter		Choose a menu with an underlined letter
Backspace		Undo the most recent change
Del	Cut all or part of an object	

Table 7.6: Key Combinations with Shift and Alt (cont.)

There are also four key combinations with the Ctrl key that have special functions (see Table 7.7).

Key Combination	Function
Ctrl-Home	Place the insertion point at the beginning of the text, or select the first object

Table 7.7: Key Combinations with Ctrl

Key Combination	Function
Ctrl-End	Place the insertion point at the end of the text, or select the last object
Ctrl-Left Arrow, Right Arrow	Place the insertion point behind or in front of the current word
Ctrl-PgUp, PgDn	Place the insertion point at the beginning or the end of the window

Table 7.7: Key Combinations with Ctrl (cont.)

Exercises in Using Basic Key Functions

Let's practice with the directory listing in the MS-DOS Executive window. Shrink the window for the first exercises.

Paging the Contents of the Window

Press the PgUp key several times and then PgDn. The contents of the window shift upward and downward page by page.

Scrolling the Contents of the Window

Press the Up Arrow and Down Arrow keys to scroll the contents of the window up or down line by line. Press the Right Arrow and Left Arrow keys to scroll the window contents sideways.

Selecting Entries

You can extend the selection bar over several entries by pressing the arrow keys in combination with the Shift key. The selected entries are highlighted. With the Shift key pressed, select some objects in the directory listing (names of files and applications). You need to hold the Shift key down the entire time. Use the spacebar to turn the selection mode on and off.

Deleting and Copying Entries

You can now delete an entry you selected in the directory listing by calling up the File menu with Alt-F and choosing the menu option Delete by pressing D. Or you can copy a file or application to another disk or directory by pressing the C key to choose the Copy option. You can also print and re-name files.

As soon as you release the Shift key and press another arrow key, the previous selection rectangles are deleted.

Canceling Actions

You can use Esc to cancel a dialog or the execution of a command, without saving your changes. For practice, call up the File Menu with Alt-F, and then choose the Get Info option by pressing G. The dialog box that is displayed disappears when you press Esc.

Ending Actions

You can use the Enter key to end an action rather than cancel it. For practice, open the File menu with Alt-F, and select the Get Info option by pressing G. Press the Enter key to end the execution of the Get Info option.

Choosing an Application Using Letters

We now show you how to call up menu options and dialog boxes by using their underlined letters.

1. Position the marker in the MS-DOS Executive window on the TERMINAL.EXE entry by pressing the T letter key. If this is not the first entry that begins with the letter T, you will have to press T repeatedly until the file is selected.

2. Press the Enter key to confirm your selection. The application window Terminal appears.

3. Choose the Configure menu by pressing Alt-C, and then press Alt-T to choose the Terminal option.

4. A dialog box appears with a list of possible responses in the dialog fields, which you can choose by using the arrow keys. In our example, the marker in the Terminal Type field jumps between the answers VT52 and ANSI.

5. You can move forward through successive dialog fields with the Tab key, and you can move backward with Shift-Tab. You can also move directly to a dialog field by pressing the letter key of the underlined letter. For practice, choose the Translation dialog field by pressing the R key.

You will see a list of different countries. Since you use letter keys to choose the various countries within the list, you can't use a letter key to switch to another dialog field. Also, you can't use a letter key in a dialog field that requires you to enter text.

6. Use Alt-B to select the dialog field Lines in Buffer. In fields with default answers, you can either delete individual characters with the Del key and add your own data, or you can simply start to add new text (the default answer will disappear). For our example, type in the digits 9 and 0. You can use the Del key or the Backspace key to correct your entry.

7. To confirm your settings, select the OK command button and press Enter. To leave the dialog box without saving the settings, press the Esc key.

Working with Multiple Windows

In Step 4, you learned the basics of working with multiple windows under the Windows program.

Activating
windows

You can make a window active with the mouse by clicking directly on the window area. When using the keyboard, you must page through the windows one at a time. Windows offers two key combinations for doing this: Alt-Esc and Alt-Tab.

When you use the second combination, an active icon is automatically opened when you release the Alt key at the moment of selection. This does not happen when you use the first combination. However, in both combinations, the active window or icon is always placed in the foreground.

You can get at covered windows more easily with key combinations than with the mouse.

An Exercise Using Multiple Windows

For this exercise, we assume that the Terminal application is active on your screen and that the Clock application is present as an icon. If this is not the case, set up your screen accordingly by using what you have previously learned.

1. Switch the Terminal application to full-screen representation with Alt-F10.

2. Switch from the Terminal to the Clock application by using Alt-Esc. Notice that the active window is indicated by a highlighted title bar.

3. Open the Clock window with Alt-Tab.

4. Return the MS-DOS Executive window to being the active application by pressing Alt-Esc twice, and then end the session with Alt-F4, Enter.

Step 8

Using the Calculator

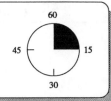

This step introduces you to the Calculator, one of the easiest Windows applications to use.

What the Calculator Can Do

The Calculator (Figure 8.1) takes up relatively little memory—only 17K—so it can be loaded automatically as an icon when Windows is started, just like the Clock. It can perform only square root and percentage calculations in addition to adding, subtracting, multiplying, and dividing. It has no parentheses function to allow you to enter a string of numbers using different operations.

Memory requirements

Figure 8.1: The Calculator application

The usefulness of the Calculator is somewhat increased by its ability to exchange input and results with the Clipboard. For

Coordinating with Clipboard

example, expressions such as 3 * 5 + 19 / 3 can be entered, and the Calculator displays the result.

The only menu for the Calculator application besides the Control menu is Edit.

You cannot change the size of the Calculator window. This restriction is indicated by the window's narrow border.

You cannot move the window with the mouse; you must use the keyboard.

Table 8.1 shows which keys and key combinations you can use with the Calculator.

Key or Key Combination	Function
M-C	Clear memory
M-R	Display memory
M-plus sign	Add to memory
M-minus sign	Subtract from memory
Ctrl-Ins	Copy to Clipboard
Shift-Ins	Paste from Clipboard
Alt-spacebar	Select the Control menu
Alt-E	Select the Edit menu
+	Add
-	Subtract
*	Multiply
/	Divide
Q	Find a square root

Table 8.1: Key Functions in Calculator

Key or Key Combination	Function
Shift-%	Find a percentage
N	Change sign (+, -)
C	Clear calculator
Esc	Clear calculator
=	Calculate result
H	Hexadecimal equivalent

Table 8.1: Key Functions in Calculator (cont.)

Starting the Calculator

To start the application, let's quickly review some of the most important and quickest Windows commands.

You can set up the Calculator application to load automatically when Windows is started by entering the following in the WIN.INI file:

```
load=calculator
```

Loading automatically

You can manually load the application as an icon in the MS-DOS Executive window by typing C to select the CALC.EXE file, and then load it with Shift-Enter.

Loading manually

To load the Calculator application as an open window in the MS-DOS Executive window, double-click on the entry with the mouse, or select it with C, and load it with the Enter key.

If you are still unsure about starting Windows and loading applications, please refer to Step 5.

Ending the Calculator

Activate the Calculator window by pressing Alt-Tab or by clicking with the mouse. End the application by pressing Alt-F4 or by double-clicking with the mouse on the Control-menu box.

Working with the Calculator

You can use the Calculator with the mouse alone, if you wish. However, if you have a computer with a numeric keypad, we recommend that you enter numbers using the keyboard. Instead of using key combinations for certain functions, you will find it easier to click on the respective icons with the mouse.

In order for the Calculator to work with the numeric keypad, you must first press the Num Lock key. When you leave the Calculator application, remember to unlock the keypad by pressing Num Lock again.

You can get instructions about using the Calculator by choosing the About Calculator option in the File menu.

Exercises with the Calculator

Multiplica-
tion and
addition

1. To practice using the basic functions, press the following keys:

   2 * 3 + 3,   Enter

   Your answer is 9.

   Now press

   3 + 3 * 2,   Enter

This time your answer is 12. The calculator pays no attention to the rule "multiplication before addition," performing its calculations strictly in the order in which they are entered.

2. To practice finding a percentage, take 25% of 400. Enter

```
400 * 25 %
```

Your answer is 100. Always multiply the number by the percentage, and then press the Percent key.

3. To practice finding a square root, take the square root of 9:

```
9, Q
```

Your answer is 3. Since there is no square root sign on your keyboard, the letter Q is used as a function symbol.

4. Finally, let's perform an exercise with the memory functions. Type the following:

```
3,M-plus sign,3*2,Enter,M-plus sign
```

You can see your result in memory by pressing M-R.

Your answer is 9. This is a way to get an answer for the first exercise that is mathematically correct. Since the calculator does not have a parentheses function, you can store intermediate results in the memory.

Step 9
Using the Cardfile

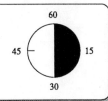

In this step, we introduce the Cardfile application, an electronic cardfile with a preset format. You will learn to make efficient use of its special key functions.

What the Cardfile Can Do

The Cardfile application itself (Figure 9.1) requires a small amount of memory, about 15K. Of course, entering information into Cardfile uses up more memory. Therefore, it is best to keep Cardfile with its data resident in memory only when working with smaller cardfiles.

Memory require-ments

Cardfile is particularly suited to managing addresses, telephone numbers, and lists. It is not possible, however, to change or enhance its preset format for entering data; the Cardfile is not a database system. You can, however, organize your entries by content.

Figure 9.1: The Cardfile application

To start Cardfile, you select and run CARDFILE.EXE in the MS-DOS Executive window.

Menus

In addition to the Control menu, the application uses the File, Edit, View, Card, and Search menus.

Files that are created by the Cardfile application have the extension .CRD.

Tips for Using Cardfile

Interfacing with other applications

The usefulness of the Windows Cardfile is increased by its ability to work in tandem with other Windows applications. You can transfer pictures from graphics programs or notes from the Notepad application and file these in the Cardfile.

Since the Cardfile and Terminal applications share common dialing functions, you can store telephone numbers and other information in Cardfile, such as user identification and operating instructions. This is helpful if you frequently work with several different electronic information services.

It allows you to retrieve the telephone number of a bulletin board system from Cardfile and then start the Terminal application. You also can use the dialing function for telephone conversations with your acquaintances and business partners.

If you plan to work for extended periods with a large number of Cardfile cards, you should switch the application window to full-screen representation or enlarge the window as we described in steps 6 and 7.

You can use the View menu to display the index lines of your cards in a list format. The index line is the bar that appears at the top of each card where you enter the text that Cardfile uses to alphabetically sort the cards. By using View, you can see a larger number of cards in a shorter time.

For very large files that can be subdivided according to subject areas, you should open separate Cardfile files for each subject. If necessary, you can combine files into one cardfile with the Merge option in the File menu.

Cardfile files

When using several different cardfiles, you should create an individual subdirectory for them with a name like Cardfiles.

If you frequently retrieve addresses from Cardfile for documents, you should file the name and address information in the customary format in the first lines of the information area, the main part of the card that sits below the index line. This makes data retrieval considerably easier.

Elements of a Cardfile

For each cardfile, you create and store a file that has an eight-character name with the extension .CRD. You can only have one file open at a time. You create additional cardfiles with the menu option New in the File menu. Cardfile cards are automatically alphabetized by the entries on the index line.

Naming conventions

The information area is separated from the index line with a line and can accept text, pictures, or a mixture of both. You select the text or picture mode.

The index line may contain several keywords separated by spaces. The insertion point always appears in the information area when you open a card and can be moved to the index line by using the Index option in the Edit menu, by using the function key F6, or by double-clicking with the mouse. You will see a dialog box in which new text for the index line can be typed or in which old text can be changed.

Typing keywords

When you type a telephone number on the index line, you should always include the necessary area codes and prefixes.

Telephone numbers

You can separate these by hyphens, for example, 212-555-6180. Numbers can be automatically dialed using the Autodial option in the Card menu.

Transferring data

The text on the index line and in the information area of a card can be freely edited. You can transfer data with the mouse or the keyboard from the index line or the information area to Clipboard. You can also transfer objects consisting of individual words and numbers from Clipboard back to both areas. Pictures and larger texts can only be transferred to the information area, where there is enough room for them.

Representing cards

In the Cardfile work area, you can either list the cards' index lines or display them on the screen as a series of overlapping cards. Only the first card is shown completely; the information areas for the other cards remain concealed. The Cardfile cards are managed like an ordinary roll cardfile. After you reach the last card, the first card appears next.

The special menu selections and key functions of the Cardfile application are described in Table 9.1.

Key or Key Combination	Function
F3	Find text string (or partial word); Find Next
F4	Go to index entry
F5	Dial the telephone number in the index line
F6	Input or change the index line
F7	Add a new card

Table 9.1: Key Functions in Cardfile

Key or Key Combination	Function
Alt-Backspace	Undo the last change
Alt-F,M	Merge two cardfiles
Alt-F,P	Print the card in the foreground
Alt-F,A	Print all cards
Alt-E,T	Switch to text mode
Alt-E,P	Switch to picture mode
Alt-E,R	Restore the previous state after a change
Alt-V,C	Switch to card representation
Alt-V,L	Switch to list representation
Alt-C,P	Duplicate a card
Alt-C,D	Delete a card
Alt-S,F	Switch the text string for Search in the information area

Table 9.1: Key Functions in Cardfile (cont.)

Working with the Cardfile

Paging

You can page through cards by using the Down Arrow, Up Arrow, PgDn, and PgUp keys, as well as by using Home and End. One peculiarity you will discover when working in Card mode is that the Ctrl key must be pressed with the Home and End keys to select the first or last card in alphabetical order.

Using the mouse

With the mouse, you can click directly on the desired card, or you can page through the Cardfile with the scroll bar. You can also select the index line to make a change by double-click-ing with the mouse.

Entering data

You type in and edit the data in the information area of the card using the keyboard. Word wrap occurs automatically. You move the insertion point with the spacebar, the arrow keys, the Ins key, and the Del key.

An Exercise Using Cardfile

1. Start Windows and the application CARDFILE.EXE. An empty Cardfile card appears on the screen.

2. Press the F6 function key, and then type the following text on the index line:

   ```
   Becker Thomas  Dr. 555-3167
   ```

   Press Enter.

3. Type in the following address in the information area:

   ```
   Dr. Thomas Becker
   123 Garden Street
   Memphis, TN 38134
   ```

4. Now create a new card with F7. Type the following on the index line:

   ```
   Hill  Kay  B. 555-1319
   ```

   Press Enter and type Hill's address in the information area:

   ```
   Kay B. Hill
   412 Haven Lane
   Boston, MA 02118
   ```

5. In the same way, create three more new cards for the following people:

```
Michael Orton, 26 Prairie Lane,
Topeka, KS 66044
913-555-2047

Claude Hellman, 1243 Festival Street,
Annapolis, MD 21430
301-555-2756

Tim Hansen, 76 Freedom Way,
Portland, OR 97203
503-555-1726
```

6. Duplicate the last card from the Card menu. This process is useful if you want to retrieve the format of a card as a template and simply type in new data. To do this in one step, press Alt-C, P.

7. Change the contents of the duplicated card. Press the function key F6 and type the following on the index line (the old text is automatically deleted):

```
Holmes   Ivan   555-6629
```

Press Enter.

8. In the information area, you can select the old information to be deleted by simultaneously pressing the Shift key and the arrow keys, or by dragging the mouse. The selected area can be deleted with the Del key, but it will be deleted automatically when you type new text.

9. Now type

```
Ivan Holmes
1419 College Lane
Santa Fe, NM
```

10. Page through the cards in your cardfile using the keyboard or the mouse.

11. For practice, switch to the list representation with Alt-V,L.

12. For further practice, search for Mr. Hellman's card by pressing F3 and typing his name as the text string.

13. Save this cardfile under the name ADDRESSES.

Step 10
Using the Calendar

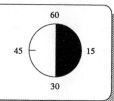

In this step, you learn about the Calendar application, an organizational tool that is like a real calendar. You can learn Calendar quickly, because it is very similar to Cardfile in the way information is entered.

What the Calendar Can Do

Without entries, the Calendar application (Figure 10.1) uses approximately 28K of memory.

Memory require- ments

You can set up CALENDAR.EXE to start automatically when Windows is started, if the Calendar doesn't have too many entries. This is useful because of Calendar's built-in alarm function, which you can use to remind yourself of upcoming appointments.

Figure 10.1: The Calendar application

You cannot change the format of the calendar display, but you can change the time divisions. For a quick orientation, switch the calendar between a day and a month view.

Files that you create with the Calendar application receive the extension .CAL.

Tips for Using Calendar

Interfacing with other applications

The calendar is indispensable because it can interface with other applications. Even if you are working in another application, a blinking alarm icon notifies you when it is time for an appointment.

Multiple calendars

If you share a PC in your company with several colleagues, or your PC is networked with other computers, a personal calendar should be kept for each person. These calendars can be displayed next to each other in separate Calendar windows to help you keep track of them.

You can also create an additional, central calendar, transferring important appointments from the personal calendars using the Clipboard.

At the beginning of the year, a work calendar for the whole company can be distributed as a Windows file, in which holidays and important company appointments have already been entered.

The space for telephone appointments is somewhat limited, for example,

```
11:30     Call Becker
```

You can get around this problem by keeping the telephone number in the Cardfile application, which you can access as an icon.

If you want to put more details in a Calendar entry, just record the name of a Notepad file, which will give you quick access to your notes.

To save space in the day view, you should periodically remove elapsed appointments using the Remove option. With the Special Time option in the Options menu, you can enter appointments for any desired time, even though the Calendar has only hourly divisions.

You can also use the early alarm function so that you will be reminded several minutes before an actual appointment.

*Early
alarm*

Elements of the Calendar

The Calendar consists of appointment areas that display a view either of a 9-hour day or the days of the month, depending on which mode you've selected. Below the appointment area is a three-line scratch pad. In the day view, you can make a short entry next to the hour bar. You can also scroll through all 24 hours with the scroll bar. In the month view, you can highlight individual days. The work area contains one appointment area at a time, and the appointment areas can be scrolled forward and backward.

The special menu options and key functions of the Calendar application are described in Table 10.1.

Key or Key Combination	Function
F4	Jump to a specified date
F5	Set/remove an alarm
F6	Turn on/off the special day marker
F7	Insert a special time in day view

Table 10.1: Special Menu Options in Calendar

Key or Key Combination	Function
Tab	Switch the insertion point between the appointment area and the scratch pad
Ctrl-PgDn	Page to the appointment area for the next day
Ctrl-PgUp	Page to the appointment area for the previous day
Alt-F,R	Remove all appointments between two dates
Alt-V,D	Switch to day view
Alt-V,M	Switch to month view
Alt-S,T	Display current day
Alt-A,S	Set or clear alarm for appointment
Alt-O,D	Change defaults for day view mode

Table 10.1: Special Menu Options in Calendar (cont.)

The Calendar uses the same positioning keys as the Cardfile: the arrow keys, the page keys, Home, End, and Enter. You can use them, in tandem with the Shift key, to select or expand entries.

The PgUp and PgDn keys work only in day view mode. They have no effect on the scratch pad.

Paging

To page through appointment areas, you must first place the insertion point in an area by pressing Tab or by clicking with the mouse.

Scrolling the day view

If the day view contains more than 10 entries, you must use the arrow keys or the mouse with the scroll bar to scroll the time bar higher or lower.

You select a day view from the month view by putting the insertion point over the date and pressing Enter. Regardless of the view representation, you can highlight the day currently being edited by pressing F6.

You can enter as many alarm times in the appointment areas as you wish by using F5. The title bar or the calendar icon will blink at the times you enter. If the Calendar application is active, a signal sounds, which can be turned off by selecting the appropriate option in the dialog box that pops up.

Setting the alarm

An Exercise Using Calendar

1. Start the Calendar application, and choose the Date option from the Go To menu. For a shortcut, you only need to press the F4 function key.

2. Enter the date 1/21/91, and confirm the entry by pressing Enter.

3. Choose the Day Settings menu option from the Options menu. Leave the interval for the hour bar at 60 minutes, and change the starting time to 6:30. Confirm this entry with OK or with the Enter key.

4. Choose the Special Time option from the same menu. Use the F7 function key, and set this special time at 12:15.

5. Choose the Insert dialog box, and enter the following on the calendar page after 12:15:

   ```
   Lunch at the lake
   ```

6. Set an alarm for this important appointment by pressing the F5 function key.

7. Make an additional entry next to 2:00 by moving the insertion point there with the Down Arrow key and typing

   ```
   Call Freddy about contract
   ```

   Set an alarm here.

8. In the same way, enter something for 3:00:

   ```
   Tennis with Jerry, Bob, and Herb
   ```

9. Switch to the scratch pad by pressing Tab, and type

   ```
   Yesterday's trip
   ```

10. Return to the day view by pressing Tab. Press F6 to highlight this day, although you will only be able to see this in the month view.

11. Move back to the previous day with Ctrl-PgUp or by single-clicking on the Left Arrow key with the mouse. After 12:00, enter

    ```
    Flight from Denver
    ```

12. Go to the scratch pad once more by pressing Tab, and type

    ```
    Take passport and draft of contract
    ```

13. Switch to the month view. You can do this by either clicking once on the date line with the mouse or by pressing Alt-V,M. Press the F6 key again so that two days in the month of January are specially highlighted. You will see that the comments for the 20th and 21st are marked.

14. Switch back to the calendar area with Tab, and use the Right Arrow key to go to the 21st.

15. Page to the next month with Ctrl-PgDn, go to the 28th with the Down Arrow key, and mark this day by pressing F6.

16. Press Tab and type the following in the scratch pad:

    ```
    Send in tax return
    ```

17. Press Tab again. Switch back to day view with the Enter key, and make this entry after 12:00:

    ```
    Call tax consultant
    ```

18. Set an alarm for this appointment by pressing F5. You should also set the early alarm. Call up the Set option in the Alarm menu with Alt-A,S, remove the default value by typing the number 5, and confirm with the Enter key.

19. Save your calendar with Alt-F,S under the name APPOINTMENTS.

20. Exit the application with Alt-F4 or by double-clicking with the mouse on the Control-menu box.

Step 11
Using the Notepad

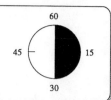

In this step, you get acquainted with the Notepad application, the "little sister" of the Write application. It is not as powerful as Write but neither does it require as much memory, which can be advantageous in some situations.

Step 12, which covers Write, builds on what you learn here in step 11, so learning Notepad is a good introduction to the basics of Write.

What the Notepad Can Do

The application NOTEPAD.EXE (Figure 11.1), without data entered into it, occupies only 10K of memory. It is intended for writing short texts for personal use and provides no text-formatting functions other than word wrap.

Memory require-ments

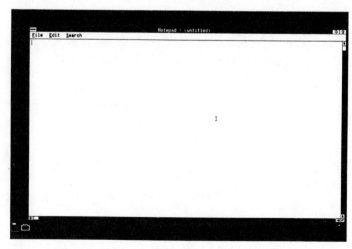

Figure 11.1: The Notepad application

Notepad is a convenient editor under Windows for system files, such as WIN.INI and AUTOEXEC.BAT. The files you create with Notepad have the default extension .TXT.

Tips for Using Notepad

You can edit texts with up to 16,000 characters in Notepad. Also, you can find out how much space is left in the work area by calling up the menu option About Notepad from the File menu.

To start Notepad indirectly when you call up certain files, you should assign the .BAT and .SYS extensions to Notepad in the WIN.INI file. When making these changes, you should first save the old contents under another name.

Menus In addition to the Control menu and the two standard menus, File and Edit, Notepad has a Search menu. In general, these menus contain only some of the options used in the Cardfile application.

If you are already familiar with Cardfile, you only need to learn the last three options in the Edit menu to work efficiently with Notepad.

Special menu options and key functions of the Notepad application are described in Table 11.1.

Key or Key Combination	Function
F3	Input a search string and continue search
F5	Insert date and time at the insertion point

Table 11.1: Special Menu Options in Notepad

Key or Key Combination	Function
Alt-Backspace	Undo the last change
Alt-F,B	Find percentage of remaining free work space
Alt-E,W	Turn on/off word wrap
Alt-S,F,M	Turn on/off uppercase/lowercase for search functions
Alt-S,F	Input text, and search after pressing the Enter key

Table 11.1: Special Menu Options in Notepad (cont.)

Working with the Notepad

You can page in Notepad and position the insertion point with the arrow keys, the page keys, Ctrl-Home, and End, or by using the mouse on the scroll bar.

Paging

You can select parts of text by dragging the mouse while pressing the left mouse button, with the keyboard by pressing the key combination Shift-arrow key, or with the Select All command in the Edit menu, Alt-E,S. Pressing an arrow key by itself cancels extended selections.

Selecting text

You can edit notes with the help of the Del key, the Backspace key, and the Ins key. Pressing the Enter key starts a new line of text. Note that inserted text is not automatically wrapped but goes off the edge of the screen, causing the window to scroll horizontally.

Editing notes

Notepad has fixed tab stops that cannot be altered. Press the Tab key to advance to the next tab stop and Shift-Tab to go backward.

Tabs

Clipboard

To copy large text passages into Clipboard, select the text and then copy it with the Ctrl-Ins command. You can paste the contents of Clipboard as often as you wish into different places in the Notepad by using Shift-Ins.

An Exercise Using Notepad

1. Start Windows, load the file WIN.INI by double-clicking on it with the mouse or by highlighting it and pressing Return, and search there for the text.

```
load=
```

Press F3, type the search string "load," and start the search by pressing the Enter key. Since "load" is on a comment line and is not the desired occurrence, press F3 once again.

2. Before you change the WIN.INI file, save it under the file name OLDWIN.INI. Press Alt-F,A. Use Home to place the insertion point at the beginning of the preset file name and type

```
old
```

When you press the Enter key, the file will be saved.

3. Add two other applications to the file WIN.INI:

```
load=clock calculator
```

Remember to insert a space between applications. (You may have already added these two in Step 5.)

4. Add the time and date. Insert a blank line by pressing Enter, move the insertion point to the beginning of the line with the Up Arrow key, and type

```
; parameters changed by the user
F5
```

5. For further practice, save this comment to the Clipboard so you can use it again. Mark the comment line by pressing Home and then Shift-Down Arrow. Save it with Ctrl-Ins.

6. Now you want to insert the contents of Clipboard into another place in the WIN.INI file. Press Alt-S,F and type the search string

```
[extensions]
```

The search begins when you press Enter, and you reach the desired occurrence by pressing F3. Now press the Down Arrow key three times, and insert the contents of Clipboard by pressing Shift-Ins.

7. To make two more entries at this position in the file WIN.INI, copy the following two lines:

```
txt=notepad.exe  ^.txt
ini=notepad.exe  ^.ini
```

First, select them by pressing Shift-Down Arrow twice, then save them to Clipboard with Ctrl-Ins. Move to the new position by pressing the Up Arrow twice, and insert the lines with Shift-Ins.

Now modify the character sequences "txt" and "ini" in these two lines to "bat" and "sys," respectively. Press the Up Arrow key twice to get to the .TXT line and press the Del key three times. Type

```
bat
```

and use Home to position the insertion point at the beginning of the line. Move to the next line by pressing the Down Arrow key. Again, delete the first three characters and type

```
sys
```

8. Finally, put another comment at the beginning of the text. Position at the beginning with Ctrl-Home. Insert a blank line with the Enter key, and use the Up Arrow key to set the insertion point on the blank line. Then type the following comment:

```
; changed version of F5
```

9. Save the new version of WIN.INI with Alt-F,S.

An Exercise Using Notepad and Calculator

If you want to check that the application Calculator is actually loaded every time Windows is started, you must first exit Windows with Alt-F,E, and then start Windows again. The icon for the Calculator application now appears at the bottom of the work area. We will use it to perform one final exercise.

1. Make sure that the Calculator and Notepad applications are in the work area. Now type the following equation in Notepad:

```
2.3 * 5.7 - 9.2 / 1.7
```

2. Transfer this equation to the Clipboard.

3. Activate the Calculator window.

4. Select the Insert command in the Edit menu. The Calculator will show the result, which you can transfer back to Notepad via Clipboard.

Step 12
Working with Write

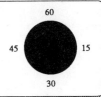

This step teaches you how to use the Write application. WRITE.EXE is a simple text processor that you can use for texts that are too large for Notepad. However, this application is considerably more powerful than Notepad and offers you valuable text-formatting functions.

This step builds on the previous step. You will find Write much easier to use if you have read the text and done the exercises for the Notepad application first.

What Write Can Do

Write (Figure 12.1) is the first document system that has been designed especially for Windows, so it makes full use of Windows' facilities. You can use Write to transfer graphics from other Windows applications and change their size.

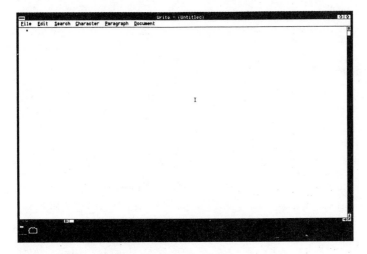

Figure 12.1: The Write application

Write makes excellent use of the Windows graphics interface in formatting text. It can display text on the screen as it will appear when printed and can even represent different fonts, font styles, and font sizes simultaneously.

Missing functions

Write's ability to work in tandem with other applications under Windows makes up for its missing functions. It does not have a spell checker or automatic hyphenation and cannot produce columns or merge files.

Write has more key combinations than Notepad for rapidly positioning the insertion point and also has a search and replace function.

Files that are created with Write have the default extension .WRI.

Tips for Using Write

To learn to use Write efficiently, you need to learn the special menu functions that enable you to manage the look of your documents.

The File Menu

You can edit large texts with Write if you have sufficient working memory. The File menu has a Repaginate option for controlling the page breaks in large texts.

Printers

You can use different printers with Write, without having to detour through the Control Panel. This is practical if you want to set up one printer for quick and inexpensive draft printing and another for high-quality printing.

The menu option Save As allows you to save text in the format of the application Word, just as it supports the loading of Word documents. However, it can be somewhat impractical to load Word files into Write because certain font-formatting features are lost. It is better to use Write to create texts for Word or for other powerful text-processing and document-formatting software, such as PageMaker or Ventura Publisher.

The Edit Menu

In addition to its normal functions for using the Windows Clipboard, the Edit menu contains commands that allow you to move pictures horizontally and to change their size. You move pictures vertically by deleting and inserting neighboring lines.

The Undo menu option restores the last change that you made.

The Search Menu

In addition to the standard options Find and Find Next, the Search menu contains the options Change and Go To Page, which make it possible to select a page directly. This helps you a lot when you edit large texts.

Selecting a page

The Change command is a special type of Search command that allows searching with and without changes. Change can also make changes automatically, thus allowing you to change all occurrences of a given pattern with a single action. This procedure can be risky, however, since Write, unfortunately, does not indicate the changes that it makes.

You can have more control by using Search and Change with selective change, which allows you to cancel undesired changes with the Undo command. Undo can reverse all the effects of a single global change. However, it cannot restore any data from changes made previous to the most recent action. Therefore, when you make a series of extensive changes, you should make backup copies of your text from time to time. You may find it practical to number these copies consecutively, for example, TEXT01.WRI, TEXT02.WRI, etc.

One practical feature of the Change dialog box is that it does not automatically disappear from the work area after you enter your search parameter.

The Change dialog box can also be moved. When you are editing a text, move the box to the upper right-hand or left-hand corner of the Write window. Then you can quickly and easily change the Search and Change patterns at any time.

The Character Menu

Fonts

The Character menu allows you to change the style of a font according to its size, type, and mode. Write offers five different print densities for the Times Roman font, which is supported by many printers. If you want to use the other fonts, check to see if the printer and the driver program you have chosen can support them.

Write allows you to use up to three fonts at the same time; the choice of fonts depends on what printer you are currently using. You can assign Bold, Italics, and Underline to whatever function keys you like. You must choose the less frequently used Superscript and Subscript from the menu.

The Paragraph and Document Menus

Formatting

Write offers you direct display on the screen of the most important formatting capabilities, such as flushing text left, flushing text right, centering text, and justifying text. Write helps you because you can see beforehand how your text will look when it is printed.

You format one paragraph at a time so that the function does not take up too much time. You create a paragraph by pressing the Enter key after you type in text. The paragraph character is not visible on the screen, but it can be found with the Search function just as with other control characters.

When you create a new paragraph, it automatically inherits the settings of the paragraph immediately preceding it. Before you enter the first line of text, you should consider the line spacing and the indentation, which are set in the Paragraph menu, as well as the page layout, which is set up in the Document menu.

With the help of the ruler bar and its symbols for text alignment and tabs, you can reformat selected groups of paragraphs by simply clicking on the symbols with the mouse.

Headers and footers, which are also typed from the Document menu, are not shown in the Write window but appear when printed.

Besides the basic function keys described in Step 7 for the Notepad application, Write uses additional keys and key combinations, which are described in Table 12.1.

Key or Key Combination	Function
F3	Find next occurrence
F4	Go to page
F5	Default character style
F6, F7, F8	Turn on bold, italic, underline
Alt-F6	Switch between Write window and Find or Change dialog box

Table 12.1: Special Menu Options in Write

Key or Key Combination	Function
Alt-Backspace	Undo last change
5-Up Arrow	Put insertion point before previous paragraph
5-Down Arrow	Put insertion point before following paragraph
5-Left Arrow	Put insertion point before previous sentence
5-Right Arrow	Put insertion point before following sentence
5-PgUp	Put insertion point back one page
5-PgDn	Put insertion point forward one page
5-Home	Put insertion point at beginning of text
5-End	Put insertion point at end of text
Ctrl-PgUp	Put insertion point at beginning of window
Ctrl-PgDn	Put insertion point at end of window
Shift-Ctrl-Home	Extend selection to beginning of text
Shift-Ctrl-End	Extend selection to end of text
Shift-Ctrl-PgUp	Extend selection to top of screen
Shift-Ctrl-PgDn	Extend selection to bottom of screen
Alt-F,H	Change active printer
Alt-F,R	Repaginate

Table 12.1: Special Menu Options in Write (cont.)

Key or Key Combination	Function
Alt-E,M	Move picture horizontally
Alt-E,S	Change picture size
Alt-S,C	Search without change, search with change, change word found, change search string
Alt-C,P	Put in a superscript
Alt-C,C	Put in a subscript
Alt-C,F	Choose font and type size
Alt-C,1,2,3	Switch current font
Alt-P,L	Align text left
Alt-P,R	Align text right
Alt-P,C	Center text
Alt-P,J	Justify text
Alt-D,H	Open header
Alt-D,F	Open footer
Alt-D,R	Turn on/off ruler
Alt-D,T	Turn on/off tabs
Alt-D,P	Set up page layout

Table 12.1: Special Menu Options in Write (cont.)

You can use all positioning commands, including those standard key combinations not listed here, with the Shift key to extend selections.

More Tips

In addition to the positioning functions already discussed for Notepad, Write uses other key combinations that help you edit text fast. You have probably already learned the combinations with the Go To key (5 on the numeric keypad).

Once you have displayed the ruler via the Document menu, you can shift the side margins with the mouse by dragging the border markers. For paragraph formatting, the following symbols are displayed in the ruler from right to left; Justification; Align Right, Centered, Align Left; single, 1 1/2 line, and double spacing; Tabs and Decimal Tabs. You can choose the symbols by clicking with the mouse.

When you make global changes in several paragraphs, you must first select the paragraphs. Besides the normal selection possibilities in Windows discussed in previous steps, Write uses the left column of the work area as a selection column. Single-clicking on the selection column selects the line next to it, and double-clicking marks the paragraph to the right. When you single-click with the Ctrl key down, the sentence that has the cursor in it will be selected.

You can delete selected text passages by pressing the Del key.

Using the Clipboard

You can exchange and copy large text passages within a document and between different documents via Clipboard. The best way to exchange several parts of a document between two documents is to load the application Write twice, and then copy the text.

An Exercise Using Write

1. Start Write by calling up the file PRACTICE.WRI in the MS-DOS Executive window.

2. Display the ruler bar, then change the page layout to Left Margin: 3 cm, and Right Margin: 3.34 cm. Set the font that you want to use.

3. Select the entire document, then choose Justified, Double Space, and Indent First Line: 1 cm, for your paragraph formatting. If you want to use the mouse, you can use the formatting symbols on the ruler. Note that the left margin for the entire document is determined by the small point on the ruler, which is located under the triangular margin delimiter for the current paragraph.

As long as you have selected the document, you can try out other format variations as well.

With the text selected, choose the Centered option, and then cancel this formatting. Your choice is once again the Justified option.

4. Copy the text that is still marked to Clipboard, and then retrieve it twice. Switch the Write window to full-screen representation.

5. Use the Change menu option in the Search menu to search for the term "to" without entering a changed term, and choose the Find Next dialog box. Move the dialog box to the right, under the ruler.

6. Continue your search with F3. When the message "The search is completed" appears, type a space for the search string and two spaces for the change instruction. Then choose the Change All mode.

7. Enter You as the next search string and You as the change instruction, and choose Change, then Find. When the first occurrence is found, turn on the character styles Bold, Italics, and Underline with F6, F7, and F8.

Now choose Change, then Find again, press F6, F7, and F8 again, and repeat until the message "The search is completed" appears.

8. Page to the beginning of the text, and call up the Header option in the Document menu. Press Enter simply once. Call up the Right option in the Paragraph menu, and choose the Insert Page # button in the Page Header dialog box.

9. Switch to the Write window with Alt-F6, press Enter once, call up the Centered option in the Paragraph menu, and type the following:

   ```
   Test printout for Write
   ```

10. Switch back to the Header dialog box with Alt-F6 and leave it with Esc. The header displayed in the text disappears, since the header is not normally displayed in Write.

As a further short exercise, call up the Repaginate menu option from the File menu. Choose Confirm Page Break from the displayed dialog box. Confirm by choosing OK, and confirm each of the suggested page breaks step by step.

Printing text

Finally, we want to look again at how to print a document. We will also insert an address from Cardfile into a document.

An Exercise Using Cardfile and Write

1. Switch to the MS-DOS Executive window, and start the Cardfile application indirectly by calling up the ADDRESSES.CRD file that you created in Step 9.

2. Copy an address to Clipboard, switch back to the Write window, and position the insertion point at the beginning of the text.

3. Type

   Mr.

and position the insertion point at the beginning of the following line, where you will subsequently copy the address from Clipboard. Press Enter three times.

4. Call up the Print command from the File menu. Choose the Draft option from the dialog box that appears. You should indicate that you want only Page 1 and Page 2 to print. After you confirm your selections, printing begins.

5. End the Write application, without saving the change to the PRACTICE.WRI file.

Step 13
Working with Paint

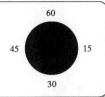

In this step you learn about the Paint application. You will find that, next to Write, it is the most comprehensive and intricate application included in the Windows package. It is different from the text-oriented Windows applications we have introduced because it arms you with numerous graphics tools.

What Paint Can Do

The PAINT.EXE application (Figure 13.1) occupies 63K of active memory, not counting the drawings you create. All versions of Paint through 2.1 can create graphics only in black and white.

Memory require- ments

Paint is designed to run with the mouse, which is especially useful in a drawing program. All Paint features, however, are accessible with the keyboard.

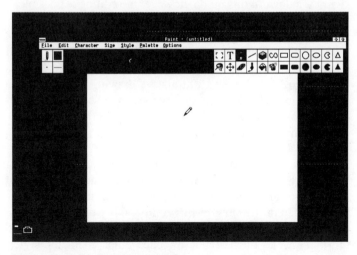

Figure 13.1: The Paint application

Graphics limitations

Although you can create bar graphs and pie charts in Paint, it does not automatically convert numerical information into these types of business graphics.

Paint does not offer graphics libraries, nor does it support precise drawings of the type required by architects and engineers.

Files created in Paint are given the default file extension .MSP.

Tips for Using Paint

Paint accepts business graphics from programs like Excel and text from the Write application, and allows you to add free-hand illustrations or change various details. You can put this touched-up work back into other Windows applications, such as Cardfile and Write.

Changing drawing size

For detailed work, you can increase the size of any part of a drawing in Paint. Or you can decrease the size of a drawing, if you want to get an overview of one that is larger than the Paint window. In this mode, however, no editing is possible.

Using high resolution

You can use the high resolution feature in Paint to sketch a logo or symbol, reduce it to the size you want in Write, and then use it in Write, Cardfile, or other applications. For example, you could create a miniature drawing of a telephone as the symbol for a phone number, or an envelope for an address. You could also use a road map created in Paint to accent an invitation in Write.

Character styles

For the most part, Paint has the same possibilities as Write for altering the appearance of individual characters, although their representation and arrangement in the menus is somewhat different. Because of this compatibility of the two applications, you are able to easily move documents back and forth between them. Paint includes other character styles, such as Outline and Strikeout. (If you move Paint text into Write, however, you cannot edit it in Write; it is treated as if it were a graphic.)

The Edit menu in Paint lacks the Size Picture feature found in Write. Instead, Paint offers the commands Erase, Invert, Trace Edges, Flip Horizontal, and Flip Vertical, which have been specially designed for editing pictures.

Editing pictures

The Palette and Options menus are used to set line width, brush shape, and the paint pattern. You can even create your own brushes and patterns. Unfortunately, Paint cannot save your custom choices in these menus.

You can zoom in on all or part of a picture, or set up an invisible grid on the drawing window for use in aligning parts of drawings.

Zooming

Before you begin drawing, you must choose from the Options menu whether you are creating the drawing for printing or for viewing on the screen. If you select For Printer, the size of the drawing window is set according to the size of paper you are using.

For sketches, you will want to choose low resolution. High resolution is desirable for precise drawings that have a lot of detail. Printing in high resolution, however, takes a longer time.

Resolution choices

You cannot alter the settings on the printer and resolution options after you have begun work on a drawing. However, you can move drawings for which you have selected different options between two Paint applications by using the Clipboard.

If the drawing area is too small for your printer selection, switch the Paint window to full-screen mode.

After working on a complicated drawing for some time, you may wish to undo several actions. However, the Undo feature only works for the most recent operation. For this reason, it is a good idea in Paint, just as in Write, to save versions of your document from time to time using consecutively numbered file names.

Tools
palette

Elements of Paint

The Paint application window contains a drawing area with a superimposed two-line bar of feature symbols. The right section of the bar is the tools palette, and the left section is the status box. Tables 13.1 and 13.2 describe the palette tools and what you can do with them.

Tool	Function
Selection Rectangle	Select a rectangular section
Text	Add or edit text
Pencil	Create a freehand drawing
Line	Draw a straight line
3-D	Create a 3-D drawing
Curve	Draw a curved line
Rectangle	Draw a rectangle
Rounded Rectangle	Draw a round-cornered rectangle
Circle	Draw a circle
Oval	Draw an oval
Freehand Shape	Draw a closed, irregular form
Polygon	Draw a polygon
Selection Net	Select an irregular area for editing

Table 13.1: Tools Palette Upper Line

Tool	Function
Scroll	Move a drawing around in the drawing window
Eraser	Erase part of a drawing
Brush	Paint an area with a pattern
Fill	Fill an enclosed area
Spray Paint	Spray paint with a pattern
Filled Rectangle	Draw a filled rectangle
Filled Rounded Rectangle	Draw a filled rectangle with rounded corners
Filled Circle	Draw a filled circle
Filled Oval	Draw a filled oval
Filled Freehand	Draw a filled irregular form
Filled polygon	Draw a filled polygon

Table 13.2: Tools Palette Lower Line

The status box is found to the left of the tools palette and is separated from it by blank space. It consists of four areas, which show your current settings. The current tool is displayed in the upper left, the current paint pattern is displayed in the upper right, the brush shape is displayed in the lower left, and the line width is displayed in the lower right.

Status box

While you are working in the drawing window, the pointer takes on the appearance of the tool you are currently using.

Choosing a tool

The easiest way to choose a tool is simply to click on it with the mouse. However, you can also choose tools by paging through the list with the Tab key or by holding down Ctrl and Shift and using the arrow keys.

Table 13.3 describes keys and key combinations you can use to access Paint's features.

Key or Key Combination	Function
F3	Choose a pattern
F4	Choose a line width
F5	Turn normal text style on/off
F6	Turn bold on/off
F7	Turn italic on/off
F8	Turn underline on/off
Del	Delete selected area
Alt-Backspace	Undo a change
Alt-E,R	Delete drawing window
Alt-E,I	Invert selected area
Alt-E,H	Flip selected area horizontally
Alt-E,V	Flip selected area vertically
Alt-E,A	Trace edges
Alt-C	Call up Character menu
Alt-S	Call up Size menu
Alt-S,O	Turn outline on/off
Alt-S,S	Turn strikeout on/off
Alt-S,L	Align text left (default)
Alt-S,C	Center text

Table 13.3: Special Menu Options in Paint

Key or Key Combination	Function
Alt-S,R	Align text right
Alt-S,P	Turn text background white
Alt-S,T	Let background show through text
Alt-P,B	Choose a brush shape
Alt-O,I	Zoom in
Alt-O,O	Zoom out
Alt-O,N	Turn off grid (default)
Alt-O,F	Lay fine grid
Alt-O,M	Lay medium grid
Alt-O,C	Lay coarse grid
Alt-O,E	Edit or create a pattern
Alt-O,P	Set drawing window for printer
Alt-O,S	Set drawing window for screen
Alt-O,L	Turn on low resolution
Alt-O,H	Turn on high resolution

Table 13.3: Special Menu Options in Paint (cont.)

Using Paint

After you choose a tool from the tools palette, the pointer takes on the appearance of the current tool. For example, if you choose the Eraser tool, your pointer becomes an eraser. As in other applications, you can move the pointer around the drawing window with the mouse or the arrow keys.

Moving a tool

If you are using the mouse, you activate a palette tool by briefly pressing the mouse button. If you are using the keyboard, you select a tool with the arrow keys and press the spacebar. Releasing the mouse button or the spacebar ends the action.

When you use the curve tool or the tools that draw irregular shapes, you click on several points in the drawing window. For example, you define a curve by clicking at the start point, dragging to the endpoint, and clicking at the apex.

If you make a mistake while you are drawing, you can undo your most recent action with the Undo command (Alt-Backspace).

You use the Scroll tool to move the drawing window around in the drawing area. The tool functions much like the scroll feature in the Control menu for Windows.

Selecting an area

To select an area in your drawing, use the Selection Rectangle tool or Selection Net tool. You use these tools to cover a rectangular- or irregular-shaped area by dragging the pointer.

Selected areas can be cut out, copied, deleted, inverted, flipped horizontally or vertically, traced with double lines, or moved. To move the selected area, simply put the pointer inside the area and drag it by holding down the mouse button or the spacebar.

Filling an area

To fill a selected area, choose one of the filled shapes in the tools palette or use the Fill tool or Spray Paint.

An Exercise Using Paint

1. Start the Paint application, and make a drawing that suits your fancy for use in later exercises.

2. Switch the Paint window to full-screen representation, select the entire drawing, and copy it into Clipboard.

3. Start a second Paint application from the MS-DOS Executive window, and choose the For Printer mode in the Option menu with high resolution.

4. Copy the picture from Clipboard into the new application, and switch this application to full-screen representation as well.

5. Use the Eraser to create an empty streak through the middle of the picture.

6. Choose the Curve tool, draw a straight line along the empty streak, and then click once more with the mouse or spacebar underneath the middle of the line.

7. Press F3 to call up the Patterns menu, and choose the pattern in the lower-right corner.

8. Choose the Spray Paint tool, and paint the blank streak until it is filled up. To do this, press the spacebar together with the Right Arrow key or move the pointer with the mouse button held down. The selected pattern will not be recognizable until you have painted over the area quite a bit.

9. Move some text into the drawing by using the Text palette tool. Position the pointer where you want text to go, and type in the text.

10. Place an empty rectangle around the text, and fill it up using the Spray Paint tool.

11. Practice using the Undo function by pressing Alt-Backspace.

12. Make the text size larger using the Size Picture function, and then bring it back to normal size.

Step 14

Using MS-DOS

You have already worked with the MS-DOS Executive window in the preceding steps—it is always the first application called up in Windows. In this step we concentrate on the application's essentials in more detail.

What MS-DOS Can Do

The MS-DOS application (Figure 14.1) occupies 13K of active memory, so it is easy to start it multiple times for various tasks. You can start other applications in the MS-DOS window, alter the current directory, and set the directory's display mode.

Memory require-ments

MS-DOS is well suited to managing files, since it allows copying, deleting, and renaming, and provides you with detailed information about files. The MS-DOS icon is an image of a disk.

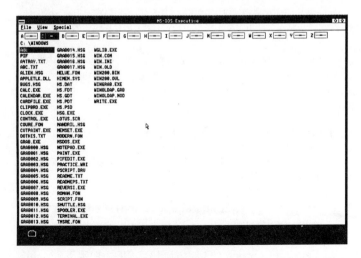

Figure 14.1: The MS-DOS application

Working with MS-DOS

The drive symbols for the available disk drives are displayed in the upper portion of the MS-DOS Executive window below the menu bar, and the current directory listing with its full path name is shown to the right of these (or below if the drives take up the whole line).

Changing drives

The disk drive currently in use is highlighted. You can change to another drive by pressing Ctrl and the disk drive's letter, or by clicking with the mouse.

Subdirectories are displayed in bold and are listed first in the directory. You select a subdirectory by double-clicking with the mouse, or by moving to it with the arrow keys and pressing Enter.

You can move to a parent directory by clicking on a portion of the path name.

Changing directories

You can change directories by using the option Change Directory in the Special menu. This menu contains additional features for creating directories and initializing disks.

In the lower portion of the work area, the contents of the current directory are displayed according to the display options in the View menu.

An Exercise Using MS-DOS

1. Start Windows. Then change the display for the directory with Alt-V,L and Alt-V,D.

2. Select the PIF (program information) subdirectory by pressing P repeatedly until it is highlighted. Press Enter.

3. Select the entries 123.PIF and BASICA.PIF. To do this,

press Shift-Down Arrow, spacebar, Shift-Down Arrow,
Shift-Down Arrow, spacebar, Alt-F, P.

4. Press Enter to confirm the file names that appear in the
dialog box. The files print.

Step 15

Using Spooler

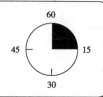

In this step, you learn about the Spooler application, which controls the printing of Windows files.

What Spooler Can Do

The SPOOLER.EXE application (Figure 15.1) can only be run once on the Windows screen. It can be started automatically whenever you print from a Windows application by setting the following parameter in the WIN.INI file:

```
spooler=yes
```

Spooler runs in the background, so you can do other things at the same time. You can break into the processing of a print job and set priorities in the queue, or even temporarily stop the print job.

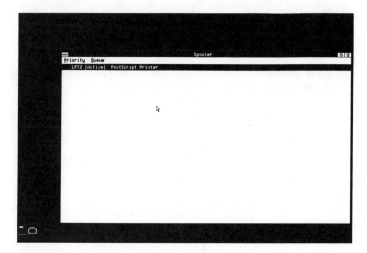

Figure 15.1: The Spooler application

Working with Spooler

The active printers are displayed in the Spooler program window along with the files waiting to be printed. By using the Priority menu, you can change the computer's scheduling for a print job by changing the priority from Low (the default setting) to High.

The Queue menu allows you to stop and restart a print job, as well as cancel it.

The icon for Spooler is an image of a printer.

An Exercise Using Spooler

1. Start Windows and call up the SPOOLER.EXE application.

2. Load the file WIN.INI from the MS-DOS Executive window.

3. Issue a print command from the File menu.

4. Change to the Spooler window, and set the print priority to High.

Step 16

Using Clipboard

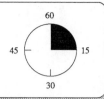

The Clipboard application is the essential ingredient in the interplay of Windows applications. You saw in the steps covering the Paint and Write applications that many features, like Paste and Copy, need the Clipboard. Yet Clipboard itself is always in the background. In this step, we give you a quick overview of the application.

What Clipboard Can Do

The Clipboard application (Figure 16.1) requires about 15K of active memory. It can only be run once on the screen and can hold only one object at a time.

Memory require- ments

You use the Clipboard to receive copies of objects or portions of objects from application windows. You can then paste these copies back into the original windows or into the windows of other applications as many times as you like.

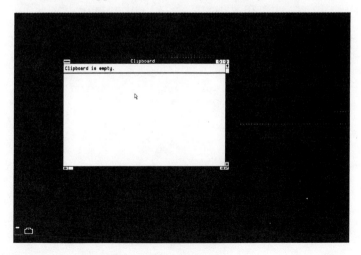

Figure 16.1: The Clipboard application

The icon for the Clipboard is an image of a board holding a note pad.

An Exercise Using Clipboard

1. Start the Clipboard and Cardfile applications.

2. Start a sample file from the Paint application.

3. Mark off a section in a drawing, and copy it into Clipboard using Ctrl-Ins.

4. Go to the Cardfile application, and choose the Picture option in the Edit menu.

5. Paste the section of the drawing you marked off into Cardfile from Clipboard.

6. Activate the Clipboard window; you will see that the section of the drawing is still present in Clipboard. (It is not erased until you copy a new drawing into Clipboard.)

7. If you like, you can now go back into the Paint window, and copy the section back into the rest of the drawing.

8. Close all the windows, without saving the changes.

Step 17
The PIF Editor

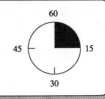

This step introduces you to the PIF Editor, which you use to set up Windows applications in program information windows.

What the PIF Editor Can Do

The application PIFEDIT.EXE (Figure 17.1) uses 24K of memory. You can use it to create new PIF files and edit existing ones. A PIF file contains all the information needed to run an application under Windows.

Memory require- ments

The abbreviation PIF is used as the icon for this application.

Working with the PIF Editor

PIF files are already furnished for most commercially available applications. If there is a PIF file for the application

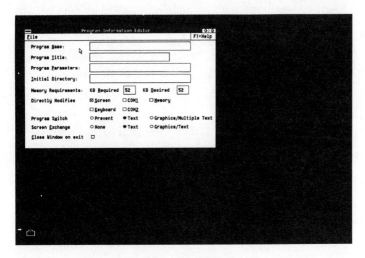

Figure 17.1: The PIF Editor application

you're working with, you need only to load this file into the PIF Editor and enter the name of the directory where you installed the application on your computer.

Creating PIF files

If no PIF file is furnished for an application, you will need to create one. You can find out how much memory the application requires by looking in the manual for the application.

Sometimes the manual does not indicate whether the application changes the memory, the video memory, the keyboard layout, the keyboard buffer, or the register and the buffer of the serial communications port. You will have to experiment to find the proper parameters.

Setting parameters

You will have to give some thought to deciding whether a program switch is possible or advantageous, and if so, whether the options Text or Graphics/Multiple text and Close Window on Exit are necessary.

Some programs, however, cannot be run in Windows at all. Others can only run with restrictions, such as no communication with the Clipboard, or full-screen representation only (that is, no window with a Control menu). On the other hand, some applications (Excel, PageMaker) that were developed especially for Windows do not need a PIF file. Windows/386 runs almost all applications; Windows/286 is more restrictive.

An Exercise Using the PIF Editor

1. Start the PIF Editor and enter COMMAND.COM in the Program Name field.

2. Under Program Title enter

   ```
   MS-DOS Commands
   ```

3. Type either C:\ or A:\ as Initial Directory, depending on

whether you want to start the program from a hard disk or a floppy disk. (If the COMMAND.COM file is not in the root directory but in a subdirectory, you must put the directory name after the backslash, for example, A:\MSDOS or C:\SYSTEM.)

4. In the Memory Requirements field, enter 52K (the default value) for both Required and Desired.

5. Check the parameters Directly Modifies: Screen; Program Switch: Text; and Close Window on Exit.

6. Save the file with Alt-F, under the name COMMAND.PIF, and leave the PIF Editor.

Now you are able to start the COMMAND.COM file by double-clicking on the COMMAND.PIF file.

Step 18

The Control Panel

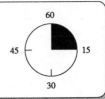

In this step you learn about the Control Panel application, which helps to set up various Windows options.

What the Control Panel Can Do

The application CONTROL.EXE (Figure 18.1) uses 18K of memory. It can only be present once as a started application in Windows. You use it after Windows is installed to set up additional printers and character styles, or to delete existing ones. You can also use it to change the settings for data communications and screen display.

Memory requirements

The Control Panel allows you to select the speed of the keyboard and the mouse, the left-handed option for the mouse button, the warning beep, and the country settings.

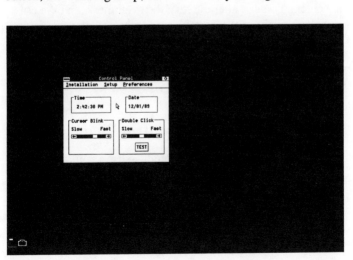

Figure 18.1: The Control Panel application

The icon for the Control Panel is an image of four windows on a screen.

Working with the Control Panel

Adding a printer

To add a printer, you must first copy a print driver into the Windows directory with the Add New Printer option in the Installation menu. The Connections option in the Setup menu allows you to connect this printer to an existing printer port or to change the port of a printer already installed.

Print parameters

The Printer menu option lets you control the number of print attempts in case of print errors, the waiting period until the printer is ready, the print format, resolution, the character-set modules, and the print colors. The Control Panel saves all these changes in the WIN.INI file.

Window parameters

The Preferences menu allows you to change the appearance of the screen. You can alter the hue, the brightness, and the color of everything from the screen and window backgrounds and the menu and title bars to the borders and the window frame.

The Country Settings menu lets you change the format of dates, times, currency, and numbers.

An Exercise Using the Control Panel

1. After starting the Control Panel, select Country Settings with Alt-P,C. Move slowly down the list of countries with the Down Arrow key, and watch how the various formats change.

2. Press Esc to leave the Country Settings dialog box.

3. Choose the Connections option in the Setup menu.

4. Use Tab to go to the Connection parameter, and choose COM1 and then "null," either with the arrow keys or by clicking with the mouse.

5. If you press Enter now, your installed printer will no longer be connected to a port. You can redirect the output to COM1 by choosing the COM1 configuration.

6. If you do not want to make any changes, press Esc or Tab to select Cancel, and press Return. This ends the Control Panel application.

Step 19
Customizing Windows

This step pulls together all the information about customizing Windows into an organized, in-depth presentation.

Making Changes to Windows

You can customize Windows to meet different needs using the installation program, the MEMSET program, and the Control Panel application, all of which make changes to the WIN.INI file. You should make your changes through these applications as much as possible, but some changes can only be made by changing the WIN.INI file directly.

Here are some of the reasons why you might decide to make changes to Windows:

- You are not content with the way in which applications run under Windows. You frequently get the message that there is not enough memory.

- The spectrum of applications you normally work with has changed.

- You have added components to your computer and want to use them efficiently under Windows.

Tips for Conserving Memory

- Leave out applications that start automatically if you seldom use them. Remove the names of these applications from the "load" and "run" parameters in the WIN.INI file.

- Turn off the Spooler program in the WIN.INI file by changing the entry

    `spooler=yes`

  to

    `spooler=no`

- Deactivate the SMARTDrive program, which increases the speed at which the disk is read, by changing the entry

    `device=smartdrive`

  in the CONFIG.SYS file.

- Put No in the PIF dialog box Program Switch to conserve memory.

- Load the biggest program first if you are working with several programs at the same time under Windows.

- Do not start memory-resident programs like SideKick, Norton Commander, and PC Tools (though these work well with Windows/386).

- Start MEMSET to control the use of memory in Windows.

Changing Disk Storage Requirements

- Delete Windows applications that you do not need any more, for example, the PIF Editor, Reversi, and Calculator.

- Regularly delete TMP files after ending Windows.

- Delete character styles (like those in Write) that you do not use any more.

- Remove print drivers that you do not use any more.

- Save applications files on additional disks.

Be sure to make a backup copy before undertaking any of these measures. You can tailor Windows with these steps so that it only requires a 1.2Mb disk drive and does not require frequent changing of disks.

Making Other Changes

If you want to use another screen adapter and/or screen mode, you must reinstall Windows.

If you want to define an output file for print jobs, enter the following in the [port] section of the WIN.INI file:

```
OUTPUT.PRN=
```

You can direct print jobs to this file from the Connection option in the Setup menu of the Control Panel application for a given printer type, including a virtual printer. You can either print them out later or use file transfer to print them from another computer.

Control Panel also controls the use of colors in Windows, the use of the mouse buttons, the setting of the button-response rate (repetition rate), and the rate at which the cursor blinks.

Step 20

The WIN.INI File

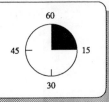

In the description of the PIF Editor in Step 17, you learned the basics of customizing Windows applications, according to your computer's capabilities. We now discuss this in more detail.

Making Entries in the WIN.INI File

You can set up special sections in WIN.INI to set parameter values for applications that are designed specifically for Windows. This generally occurs automatically or via special menus inside the applications.

As you know, PIF files are created for MS-DOS applications through the PIF Editor. However, some entries must be made directly in the WIN.INI file.

To indicate a particular file type in the MS-DOS Executive directory, you must add the type after the "program" parameter in the [windows] section of the WIN.INI file.

For example, you must add the following to handle .SYS files:

```
programs=com exe bat sys
```

After its initial use, the application Write automatically creates an [MSWrite] section with parameter settings that you can modify. For example, you can set

```
Backup=1
```

to get automatic, intermediate backups.

As described in Step 5, you can automatically load an application as an open window or as an icon by adjusting the parameter values for "run" and "load." In Step 11 you learned how to start applications by using their file types.

By combining these two options, applications that load specified files along with them can be started automatically.

The entries

```
run=appointments.cal
```

and

```
load=diary.txt
```

start the application Calendar with the file APPOINTMENTS and the application Notepad with the file DIARY.

For programs that run in a window, that are located in the root directory, and that need no keyboard, screen, or memory modifications, you can make a direct entry in the [pif] section without using the PIF Editor. To do this, you simply need a line with the following information:

```
programname.typ=required memory in bytes
```

You can temporarily leave full-screen programs like Word and change to another window by pressing Alt-Esc after the Exit command.

If you frequently work with large files, you can use the PIF Editor to reserve sufficient memory.

Index